BECKS

BECKS

The unofficial and unauthorised biography of
DAVID BECKHAM
by David Knight

Published by
Kandour Ltd
1-3 Colebrook Place
London N1 8HZ

This edition printed in 2004 for
Bookmart Limited
Registered Number 2372865
Trading as Bookmart Ltd
Blaby Road
Wigston
Leicester LE18 4SE

First published June 2004

ISBN 1–904756–05-0

Production services:
Metro Media Ltd

Author: David Knight

With thanks to: Jenny Ross, Emma Hayley,
Lee Coventry, Paula Field

Cover design: Mike Lomax
Cover Image: Rex Features

Inside Images: Rex Features

© Kandour Ltd

Printed and bound by Nørhaven Paperback, Denmark

DAVID BECKHAM

This series of biographies is a celebration of celebrity. It features some of the world's greatest modern-day icons including movie stars, soap personalities, pop idols, comedians and sporting heroes. Each biography examines their struggles, their family background, their rise to stardom and in some cases their struggle to stay there. The books aim to shed some light on what makes a star. Why do some people succeed when others fail?

Written in a light-hearted and lively way, and coupled with the most up-to-date details on the world's favourite heroes and heroines, this series is an entertaining read for anyone interested in the world of celebrity. Discover all about their career highlights – what was the defining moment to propel them into superstardom? No story about fame is without its ups and downs. We reveal the emotional rollercoaster ride that many of these stars have been on to stay at the top. Read all about your most adored personalities in these riveting books.

DAVID BECKHAM

CONTENTS

DAVID BECKHAM

FACT FILE

Full name: David Robert Joseph Beckham
Date of birth: 2 May 1975, Leytonstone
Parents: Sandra and Ted
Sisters: Lynne and Joanne
Star sign: Taurus
Height: 6' 0"
Wife: Victoria Caroline Adams Beckham
(4 July 1999 – present day)
Children: Brooklyn Joseph Beckham
born 4 March 1999 and Romeo Beckham
born 1 September 2002

Manchester United career (1991–2003)
Signs as trainee: 8 July 1991
Signs as professional: 22 January 1993
First Team Debut: v. Brighton & Hove Albion (a),
23 September 1992
FA Premiership appearances: 265
FA Premiership goals: 62
FA Cup appearances: 19
FA Cup goals: 5
UEFA Champions League appearances: 81
UEFA Champions League goals: 15

DAVID BECKHAM

Honours

1 FA Youth Cup (1992)

6 FA Premiership (1995-96, 1996-97, 1998-99, 1999-2000, 2000-01, 2002-03)

2 FA Cup (1996, 1999)

1 Champions League (1998-99)

Spanish Super Cup (2003)

England career

Full debut: v Moldova (a) 1 September 1996

First game as England captain: v Italy (a) 15 November 2000

Personal honours

PFA Young Player Of The Year 1997

European Player Of The Year (2nd place) 1999

World Footballer Of the Year (2nd place) 2000

BBC Sports Personality Of The Year 2001

FIFA World Footballer Of The Year (2nd place) 2001

Order of the British Empire (OBE), awarded 13 June 2003

1

The Galactico

DAVID BECKHAM

THE GALACTICO

Becks. Football hero, captain of England, idol to millions all over the world – the most talked about and most photographed sportsman on earth.

He earns millions for the sport he plays, and many millions more for the products he endorses. On the field he is a great player. Off the field he is courteous, polite.... and drop dead gorgeous.

Probably the most famous man in Britain – Prime Minister Tony Blair would have to settle for second place – and probably the most popular. He is a footballer and family man who is also an iconic figure around the world. All things to all men and women, his appeal reaches way beyond the range

THE GALACTICO

of even the world's most popular sport.

David Beckham is, however, no stranger to controversy; his incredible career has been laced with events of high drama. He has gone from teen idol to national villain to national hero, all within a few short years. He has his doubters who question his considerable talent with a football and his temperament, but he has always come back to prove them wrong, becoming ever more respected, popular and idolised.

Ever since his romance and marriage to pop star Victoria Adams of the Spice Girls – aka Posh Spice, he has lived his life in the glare of publicity. The rollercoaster of fame has brought highs and lows, adulation and criticism. It has never appeared to worry him.

But in the spring of 2004, David Beckham had reason to be worried....

In early April the world was in its usual state of turmoil. The British government was in hot water about its handling of the asylum seeker crisis. A year after the overthrow of Saddam Hussein, Iraq was gripped by violence and the European Union was preparing to extend its borders to welcome 10 more countries into its membership.

And all over Europe the football season was

THE GALACTICO

moving towards its climax, before the summer's big tournament of international football, Euro 2004. In England, Arsenal was pulling away from nearest challengers Chelsea and Manchester United. In Scotland, Glasgow Celtic had had the SPL championship in their pockets for months. In Italy AC Milan were also holding a clear lead over their rivals.

In Spain things were really hotting up. Real Madrid who had been leading the Spanish First Division, known as La Liga, by a long way, were being caught by rivals like Valencia and arch-enemies Barcelona. Real Madrid's recent stumbles included a defeat in the Spanish Cup Final.

At the beginning of April, Real Madrid had a single point lead over Valencia. Real Madrid was showing signs of mortality.

Known as the Galacticos, Real's current amazing line-up of superstar players, represent the cream of the world's footballing talent. Prized from Europe's other top clubs in the past few seasons, Portuguese winger Luis Figo, French midfielder Zinadine Zidane and Brazilian striker Ronaldo have joined long-term stars, like forward Raul and Brazilian left-back Roberto Carlos. The team contains perhaps the greatest array of football talent

THE GALACTICO

ever seen in a single team – or at least since the great Real Madrid team of the Fifties. The most recent big addition to their ranks, in his first season with Real is one David Robert Joseph Beckham.

Beckham proved to be a sensation for Real Madrid in his first few months of the season. His performances for the team gained rave reviews from the notoriously hostile Spanish sports media, and he was greeted with adulation by Real Madrid's notoriously difficult-to-please supporters.

But soon, Beckham like some of his illustrious teammates, is beginning to look jaded. Unlike at Manchester United, where he was rested for a few games in order to keep him fresh and injury-free, he has played in virtually every Real match – Spanish League, Cup and UEFA Champions League – in a new, more demanding role of central midfield. The rumours soon began – will Beckham be sold at the end of the season?

But worse – much worse – was about to happen. The dramas he had been through in the past – the aftermath of the 1998 World Cup, being handed the England captaincy, finally leaving United for a new career at Madrid – had been largely about football. But for the first time, it was getting personal and threatened to go straight to

THE GALACTICO

the heart of his marriage to Victoria, casting a huge shadow over their lives and their lifestyle.

On Sunday 4 April 2004 the latest bombshell in a life of high drama arrived and it came courtesy of the *News Of The World*. The front page headline 'Beckham's Secret Affair' rocked the nation. The story alleges a relationship – conducted both in person and by a series of steamy text messages via mobile phone – between David Beckham and Ms. Rebecca Loos, a former employee of Becks' former sports agents.

When photos of Becks and Rebecca together made British tabloid front pages that month, Ms Loos was soon removed from her duties. The paper duly printed the salacious content of some of their 'conversations' – with numerous words, and even whole passages, represented only as asterisks. It made, without question, dynamite reading.

On the day the story broke Posh and Becks were apart – not an unusual occurrence since Becks moved to Madrid. Victoria was at 'Beckingham Palace', their palatial home in Hertfordshire preparing to leave on a skiing holiday in an exclusive Swiss resort with her family – including her parents Tony and Jackie, her sister Louise and her husband, as well as her children Brooklyn and

THE GALACTICO

Romeo. At Heathrow, later that day, the group ran the gauntlet of photographers and become involved in a minor scuffle, before they flew out.

Becks was in Madrid and later that day a spokesman for the star released a statement about the allegations, describing them as "ludicrous... The simple truth is that I am very happily married, I have a wonderful wife and two very special kids." He then flew out to be at Posh's side.

Over the next few days, several photocalls were set up to suggest that all was well between Posh and Becks. But this was played out against an orchestrated campaign of further allegations by Loos herself – who was apparently not behind the original 4 April story but was now selling her story to the newspapers and TV. And then, the following Sunday the *News Of The World* revealed a new girl, who claimed she had been close to Becks' since they met on a Man United pre-season tour to the Far East in 2001.

The Beckham camp issued a further statement dismissing the new allegations. But a new (harsh) light was already shining on Posh and Becks' relationship and on David himself. Were there problems within the Beckhams marriage? Had they begun after, or even existed,

THE GALACTICO

before his move to Madrid? Certainly Victoria and the children had not made a permanent move to Spain as had been expected. She had preferred to concentrate on her careeer as a pop star, and spend time – in both London and New York – with the hip-hop producer-cum-entrepreneur Damon Dash.

Despite all the speculation, Posh and Becks' public displays of affection and togetherness continued. Whether part of 'Brand Beckham' or the real Becks, he has always showed himself to be a new breed of male: non-macho, non-threatening, a considerate, loving husband to Victoria, a doting father of Brooklyn and Romeo, a role model to the new generation of men who are not afraid to show their feelings and love for their family, not bothered about being 'one of the lads', not afraid to reveal their sensitive, even feminine side.

How would these allegations square with his image in the eyes of his army of adoring fans, male and female? To them he is a hero of modern times, representing the best of what the world values as the most important things in life: a brilliant sportsman, great looking, wealthy, but also a wonderful husband to his wife and father to his children.

DAVID BECKHAM

THE GALACTICO

He has been portrayed in Christ-like poses, even as a Hindu God – would he now become a fallen idol? And what impact would this have on his sponsors, his multi-million pounds-worth of endorsements?

What about the rest of this crucial season, with Real Madrid and then with England at Euro 2004. Would he be able to keep his game together? Most importantly of all, could he repair the evident damage to his marriage to Posh?

Earlier in 2004 Becks had been filmed while he was sleeping during a siesta in Spain. Shot by photographer/artist Sam Taylor-Wood and shown as part of an art exhibit, he looked beautiful and content, but was he sleeping so peacefully now? He had faced challenges before, but this was perhaps his greatest of all.

2

The early years

DAVID BECKHAM

THE EARLY YEARS

David Robert Joseph Beckham was destined to be a professional footballer. More than that, he was destined to play for Manchester United.

He was born on 2 May 1975, in Leytonstone, East London, the second child of Ted and Sandra Beckham, a couple who had married five years earlier, in London's East End, and were already proud parents of a little girl, Lynne.

Ted, a gas fitter by trade, was passionate about football, and a fair player himself. A bustling centre forward, he had trials with his local league team, Leyton Orient, and enjoyed a couple of years as a semi-pro in non-league football. But like the vast majority of youngsters who dream of playing soccer professionally, he never quite made the grade.

Ted continued to play at local level before and after David's birth – but it was soon clear that his son had not only inherited his father's huge enthusiasm for football, he also had a far greater natural talent to play the game. In the classic fashion of most successful players, he could kick a ball virtually before he could walk. From then on, he was playing football almost constantly, enthusiastically encouraged by his loving parents – particularly Ted.

Eventually Ted hung up his own boots to devote more time to his son. It was Ted who coached David in the qualities that have characterised his strengths as a player ever since: good technique, instant ball control, accurate passing, and an ability to combine individual skill and teamwork. It was Ted who allowed him to spend hours practising free kicks and corners, when he should have been in bed. And it was Ted who protected the extraordinary self-belief and appetite for the game, which young David evidently had from the start.

But together with passing on his passion for 'The Beautiful Game', Ted Beckham also instilled in

THE EARLY YEARS

his son a devotion for Manchester United. Ted was a 'Cockney Red'; part of a particular phenomenon in English football in the Sixties where relatively large numbers of Londoners came to support a team from the north of England. The Manchester United of Bobby Charlton, Denis Law and George Best was the most exciting and glamourous team in the country and the first English winners of the European Cup.

It meant that during a football-filled childhood, David quickly came to share his dad's fanaticism for United. He was soon dreaming of some day playing for the Red Devils – even though his mum's father, his beloved granddad Joe, was a die-hard Tottenham Hotspur fan, and gave him a Spurs kit every Christmas to go with the Man U kit that he received from his parents.

At the age of five, David had gained another sister, Joanne. The family had moved to Chingford, further out into East London suburbia and David was attending Chase Lane Primary School. He spent virtually all his spare time in Chase Lane Park round the corner from his home playing football, usually with much bigger boys.

He was playing in his school team, of course – and the Cubs. But more significantly, from the

THE EARLY YEARS

age of seven he was also playing for the Sunday league side Ridgeway Rovers. Over the next few years, Ridgeway swept all before them, and David was their diminutive star performer, already whipping in crosses from the right wing in the manner that would become his trademark.

Ridgeway Rovers was established by Stuart Underwood, who became the next major influence on David's development as a soccer player. He had a huge presence – partly because he was 6 foot four – but he was also a hard taskmaster and very driven about creating a successful team.

Ridgeway were exceptionally well organised on and off the pitch. After trouncing most of the local opposition, the team went on several tours abroad, playing in tournaments in Germany and Holland. Many of London's top professional players, like Spurs' striker Clive Allen, often attended Ridgeway's awards nights and impeccable standards of dress and behaviour were required from the youngsters for these events, as well as for their numerous cup final appearances.

In fact, the Ridgeway kids seemed to be in training for all the obligations the professional game would require of them. Hardly anyone felt the need to leave Ridgeway to join the London

DAVID BECKHAM

THE EARLY YEARS

professional clubs when their scouts came to see the talent on display at Ridgeway. The team stayed together for six years, and several boys eventually did become professional players. There is no doubt that the rules and discipline demanded at Ridgeway stood the young Beckham in good stead when he eventually moved to United.

Not that David really exhibited any wild tendencies that needed to be curtailed at an early age. He was an ordinary boy, not boastful about his football exploits, or temperamental. At home, he was ever the dutiful son – his main daily task was to lay the table for the evening meal, and he regularly helped his mum, a hairdresser, by making tea when she was cutting hair at home. And perhaps in another expression of the perfectionism he practiced in his football, he was unusually tidy for a young lad, keeping his room neat, and even folding his dirty washing!

Even at this tender age, he was already quite particular about his personal appearance – and had that now-familiar flamboyant streak. David has written about how, at about six-years-old, he was chosen to be a pageboy for a wedding, and picked out a very snazzy outfit, featuring maroon knickerbockers and waistcoat, frilly white shirt

THE EARLY YEARS

and ballet shoes. Much to the horror of his folks, he wanted to wear it all the time.

David went to football matches from an early age with his dad, including several Wembley Cup Finals, and games at Spurs' home White Hart Lane with granddad Joe, often when Manchester United was the visiting side. Mum Sandra put in almost as many hours with Ridgeway as his dad, driving him and numerous team-mates to games, when Ted was at work. At 11, Beckham moved to the senior school, Chingford High, where the boys played rugby not soccer.

David and several other boys soon talked the rugby teacher, John Bullock, into starting a football team and soon they started winning inter-school trophies. That was an important step; because playing for a school team meant that David could go on to play representative football for Waltham Forest District, and then Essex at county level.

He was also coming to the attention of big London clubs, like West Ham, Arsenal and Tottenham. But what he was waiting for – praying for – was that approach from Manchester United. And that was by no means certain. United certainly had fans in London – but when did they recruit their young players from London? It hardly ever happened.

DAVID BECKHAM

THE EARLY YEARS

Eventually David had to choose a professional club to train with and he chose Spurs, joining a group including Nick Barmby and Sol Campbell. He turned up to training in his Manchester United kit.

David Beckham had already set foot on the pitch at the home of Manchester United, Old Trafford. He had already been a winner at Old Trafford. And believe it or not, the away team's supporters at Old Trafford had already booed him.

It happened when he was just 11-years-old. He was taking part in a Soccer Skills school run by Bobby Charlton, the legendary footballing hero of Manchester United and England. It was the second year that David had entered Charlton's summer school – Granddad Joe paid the sizeable fee to attend – which included a skills competition. The winners of each week's competition went to on a grand final, the latter part of which took place on the Old Trafford turf, a few minutes before kick-off of a Saturday league game.

Ironically, United were playing Joe's beloved Tottenham Hotspur that day in late 1986, and when David ran out onto the pitch he was introduced to the rapidly-filling stadium as "from Leytonstone", drawing cheers from the Spurs contingent. But when the announcer added: "And David is a massive

THE EARLY YEARS

United fan" their cheers quickly turned to jeers.

In a remarkable foretaste of his future career, the youngster, faced with the personalised abuse by a section of the crowd, remained impressively undaunted. He performed superbly, winning the skills competition for his age group easily. Eventually the Tottenham fans as well as the United ones were generous in their applause at his success. It was perhaps the first example of what he has done throughout his career – winning over his numerous detractors using a combination of determination and skill.

Bobby Charlton then described David as the most skillful player of his age he'd ever seen, so perhaps it was not so surprising that United's London-based scout Malcolm Fidgeon caught up with young Beckham playing for Waltham Forest some months later. Fidgeon was impressed, and the same day he spoke to Sandra and Ted. From that moment, the Beckham family's long-held dream started to become a reality. A few days later, Fidgeon was driving David up to Manchester to play in a trial at the club.

A while later came a call to the Beckham home from Alex Ferguson, the Manchester United manager. He spoke to Ted and made it crystal

THE EARLY YEARS

clear that the club was very interested in signing young David. From that moment David was welcomed fully into the Man U set-up, and grabbed every opportunity to get involved.

With an almost touching naivety, David started to attach himself to the club, travelling up to Manchester with Fidgeon, then meeting up with the first team when they played in London, attending pre-match meals and helping the kit man clear dressing rooms after games. He was even made mascot for a fixture at nearby West Ham, and sat on the bench.

He was hanging out with his heroes, such as Bryan Robson and Gordon Strachan, and all with the encouragement of his parents and Alex Ferguson, who was clearly impressed by the young lad. At that stage, the ambitious, driven Scot was just starting out on his epic, legendary career at the helm of United. Having achieved success north of the border as boss of Aberdeen, he hoped to emulate that success at United by following the long-held tradition of the club built by the legendary Matt Busby in the Fifties and Sixties: by developing the club's own youthful talent into great football stars.

In the mid-Eighties Tottenham were a more successful team than United, as well as being the

THE EARLY YEARS

team down the road from his home. While David was training with the north London side he was offered a schoolboy forms contract by manager Terry Venables. Although the offer was very tempting David and Ted politely requested time to consider. They had every reason to think a similar offer was forthcoming from United.

And on David's 13th birthday, 2 May 1988, David was invited to United's home game against Wimbledon where, after the match he was offered a contract (two years schoolboy forms, two years YTS, two years professional) for him to sign, plus a birthday cake. Alex Ferguson produced a pen that David had bought him, and from that day, and for the next 15 years, he was a Manchester United player.

For the next two years he travelled constantly between London and the north-west, staying in Manchester throughout his school holidays in order to train and play with other Man U schoolboy hopefuls or attend first-team games. He would stay in Manchester, sharing with other boys in halls of residence, all through the summer holidays while others maybe came for just a week or a fortnight. During that time he was under the tutelage of Nobby Stiles, another United legend and World Cup winner with England.

DAVID BECKHAM

THE EARLY YEARS

But it was not until he left school and joined United full-time that the real business began. He was slowly assimilated with other youngsters who were to become the greatest crop of home-grown talent that Manchester United had produced since the Busby Babes of the Fifties.

But to begin with, it was not easy for David, and a boy without his inner confidence may have struggled. His fellow trainees were largely local lads, who he had not mixed with during his holiday visits to United.

It took Beckham a while to make friends with these young players. The team fully bonded on a trip to Ireland, where the United youngsters played and won a tournament called the Milk Cup. It was their first ever trophy as a team, and by the end of David's first season as a trainee they had shown their true potential by prevailing over every youth side in the country by winning the FA Youth Cup.

And soon after, David Beckham was receiving his own first taste of the big time. In September 1992, age 17, David was named as a substitute for a League Cup-tie at Brighton & Hove Albion. With about 20 minutes to play, he came on for his first ever appearance for the United first team.

3

The big breakthrough

DAVID BECKHAM

THE BIG BREAKTHROUGH

Considering his height and physique now, it may be surprising to learn that David Beckham was actually small for his age until he reached his late teens. Some even considered him too frail to succeed as a professional footballer. Certainly this appears to be a major reason why he was passed over for a place at the F.A. School of Excellence at Lilleshall, considered to be the finishing school for future top players.

Not that it is likely David would probably have accepted a place at Lilleshall anyway. Being at United was a dream come true. But perhaps his late physical development came in useful in some

THE BIG BREAKTHROUGH

ways. Back at Chingford High, when his school friends had been experiencing the usual teenage distractions, David had been still been entirely focused on his football. While they were going out, meeting girls and staying up late, he was at home and getting a good night's sleep.

His determination to become not only a pro footballer but a Manchester United player was total, despite knowing he knew he was considered too fragile to succeed – he was still smaller than his 5'4" mum Sandra was when he went to United full-time. He tried various methods to build himself up, even following the advice of his childhood hero at United, the all-action skipper Bryan Robson (himself an undersized young teen) who used to eat a raw egg every day.

But the fact remains that after that first appearance at Brighton in September 1992, he did not have a sniff of the first team for a long time – nearly two seasons in fact – and that was very largely due to his size. Meanwhile, other members of the so-called Class of '92, the Man United youth team that won the FA Youth Cup that year, were successfully breaking into United's senior squad.

The Class of '92 contained a truly remarkable collection of players, which included future United

THE BIG BREAKTHROUGH

heroes like Paul Scholes, Gary Neville, and Nicky Butt, Robbie Savage (now at Birmingham City) and Keith Gillespie (now at Leicester City). A year older, and the youth team captain, was Ryan Giggs. Later on Alex Ferguson described Beckham's year of trainees as "the best crop I have had in my management career."

They were trained by youth team coach Eric Harrison, the hard taskmaster who kept the youngsters' feet firmly on the ground. The fact that part of their duties were, in the age-old tradition of football apprentices, to clean the senior players' boots, the changing rooms and the showers certainly helped them stay grounded. Harrison was the next major figure in the development of Beckham's career. Hugely demanding yet encouraging, he valued honesty, respect and team spirit above all else, and those virtues shone through that brilliant young team.

The other trainees, particularly the local Manchester lads, took a little while to accept the boy from London. They regarded him suspiciously as "the flash cockney" – and they were not referring to his silky skills with a football. Nor was he particularly chatty – quite the opposite in fact. Their taunts had referred to more to do with the

THE BIG BREAKTHROUGH

obsessive attention he paid to his appearance: he was always immaculately turned out with the best kit, boots and tracksuit. (something David has attributed to having befriended kit man Norman Davies when he had helped him clean out dressing rooms as a kid). His sartorial obsession extended off the pitch, even back then.

When he became a trainee, the club had put David into digs in Manchester, when he became a trainee, but it had taken a while before he was placed with two different families before he found his ideal place with Annie and Tommy Kay. They provided home comforts, a warm atmosphere and good food for David, and they lived virtually next door to The Cliff, then the United training ground, which was very handy for a boy who had some trouble raising himself in the morning. But it was even better than that: David was eventually given the room formerly occupied by Mark Hughes, Man United's then centre forward, and one of Beckham's all-time idols.

Annie Kay, who had taken United boys for many years, later revealed that whereas other boys arrived with one or two suitcases of clothes, David arrived with several. The other thing that set him apart was that he was meticulously tidy and perfectly willing to clean his own room.

David's other big interest was fast cars – a passion he had developed as a boy, playing Scalectrix at home in Chingford. He bought his first car from Ryan Giggs when he passed his driving test – a souped-up Ford Escort. Then it was a VW Golf – with personalised number plates. No doubt he took a fair bit of flak in the dressing room for that, and also later when he upgraded his first sponsored club car, a Honda Prelude, with leather seats and alloy wheels at his own expense – even though the car would eventually be returned to the dealers.

He could hold his own in the dressing room. More importantly, he could take all the jibing with good humour – just as well, as he would have to put up with a fair bit of it in years to come.

David's big pals at that time were Ben Thornley, Chris Casper, John O'Kane and Gary Neville, as well as Gary's younger brother Phil and Dave Gardner, both playing for United's junior side at the time. The Nevilles and Gardner have remained among his closest friends, particularly Gary, who would later become his best man at his wedding as well as his right flank partner for United and England.

Becks and Nev found they had a lot in common: a similarly strong family background, and

THE BIG BREAKTHROUGH

a similar outlook. They were both fairly serious – although David was perhaps not quite as serious as Gary, who always seemed mature beyond his years – and of course absolutely dedicated to their chosen career, and their employers.

They spent many afternoons at the snooker club, but Becks and Nev often returned for some evening training with the younger recruits. Their regular weekly nights out were on Wednesdays, when they would go to a club in Manchester, and everyone would invariably end up back at Thornley's parents house, sleeping on the floor.

During his days at Old Trafford had his first real girlfriend. According to his recent autobiography (My Side), David went out with a girl called Deana for nearly three years. As well as appearing to be his first real romance it was also, with his own family far away, another way of sampling enjoying a comforting family atmosphere – he evidently enjoyed spending a lot of time at Deana's parents house, discussing football with her father who was a big Liverpool supporter.

But at United David was having a relatively frustrating time. Although he signed professional forms with United on 23 January 23 1993, a few months before his 18th birthday, other boys

DAVID BECKHAM

THE BIG BREAKTHROUGH

appeared to be leaving David behind. While he returned to the youth team (United were FA Youth Cup runners up in '93) and then the reserve team (again winners of their league), Paul Scholes, Nicky Butt, Gary Neville, even Phil Neville, two years younger than Becks, started turning out for the first team. It was a worrying period for David. There may even have been a brief moment when he doubted if he had a future at Old Trafford.

There was a general feeling that David was just too fragile to compete at the highest level. He needed toughening up, and that was something youth coach Eric Harrison worked on constantly. But finally, at the beginning of 1995, Alex Ferguson took matters into his own hands.

In December 1994, David had actually played for the first team at Old Trafford Trafford in a Champions League game against Turkish side Galatasary, even scoring his first senior goal for the club. But a short while later Ferguson informed Becks that he was shipping him out of Old Trafford to Preston North End, then in the Third Division – on a month's loan.

David was initially devastated. Was the club he loved about to ditch him? Ferguson calmed his fears: this was not the first stage towards the exit

THE BIG BREAKTHROUGH

door from Old Trafford. But it was a real test – could he survive in the full-blooded, uncompromising combat of basement league football? How would he fare against no-nonsense (and often no-skill) defenders and their crunching tackles?

In fact, his time at Preston North End did wonders for Beckham's development, and he has described it as, in some ways, the making of him as a player. For the first time he fully experienced the competitive edge of league football, and the huge will to win expressed by his new teammates. More importantly he was also able to display his talents, and gain that important vital boost of confidence.

David actually scored on his league debut, for Preston against Doncaster, direct from a corner. He scored another in the next game against Fulham, this time in the style that was to become his trademark, from a long-range free kick. By the end of the month's loan he would have been happy to stay at Preston for longer. But his manager back at United had other ideas. David Beckham was about to join the first team set-up at Manchester United good and proper.

In fact a big shock was in store for the football world as Ferguson effectively dismantled the team that he had created to bring the League Championship to Old Trafford for the first time

THE BIG BREAKTHROUGH

in 25 years. He wanted to make more room for the talented youngsters known as 'Ferguson's Fledglings', and in the summer break of 1995, after United had been pipped to the title by Blackburn Rovers, Ferguson controversially dispensed with the services of three senior players: Mark Hughes, Paul Ince and Andre Kanchelskis.

The departure of Hughes and Ince was particularly surprising, that of Kanchelskis less so, as it was known he had fallen out with 'the gaffer'. But it was Kanchelskis's removal that was most significant for David Beckham because they played in the same position wide right of midfield.

David had actually made his league debut for United at home to Leeds United towards the end of the 1994–95 season, just after his spell at Preston, and had since played three further times. And when the 1995–96 season began with an away fixture at Aston Villa, Becks came on as sub to join Scholes, Giggs and Neville. He scored too – his first Premiership goal for United – but this was just a consolation effort in a comprehensive 3–1 defeat. The game was perhaps more significant for the reaction it provoked, especially when the highlights of the game were shown on *Match Of The Day* that evening.

DAVID BECKHAM

THE BIG BREAKTHROUGH

The verdict on the new United team by pundit Alan Hansen – a multi-title winner as a Liverpool player numerous times – was damning. "You never win anything with kids," he declared. But the respected Hansen would come to regret making that memorable pronouncement, because United were about to experience one of their most successful domestic seasons ever, with those kids.

After that first defeat, they won five straight games, including a 2–1 victory at Blackburn where David scored the winner. That kept them in touch with their leading rivals that year, Newcastle United, who had had a terrific start. But at one stage Man United were 12 points behind Newcastle, who looked certainties for the Premiership title, and although Newcastle's form faded at a crucial point of the season, it took an extremely determined Man U to claw back the deficit.

The star, without question, was Eric Cantona, the enigmatic and brilliant French striker. Having returned a few games into the season from a lengthy suspension, Cantona was the team's inspiration and the goal-scorer in a remarkable sequence of 1–0 victories. But David was a regular in that side, playing 33 out of 38 games, scoring seven times, and giving the first indication to the public at large of his

THE BIG BREAKTHROUGH

remarkable ability with the ball.

Man United won the 1995–96 Premiership title on the final day of the season. Alex Ferguson's brave gamble had been vindicated and David Beckham had his first Championship medal. And the season was not over yet: there was still an FA Cup Final to play, against Liverpool. In the semi-final against Chelsea, David scored the goal that took Man U to Wembley. Now he was going to play in one.

There was high expectation of an exciting game between two huge rivals bristling with talent. The reality was, as a football spectacle, extremely disappointing. But as it looked certain that the tedious contest would be extended into extra-time Beckham took a corner from the left, which was half cleared and Cantona – who else? – poked the ball back through a crowd of players into the net. A few minutes later Cantona (also skipper) collected the FA Cup and Manchester United had completed their second League and Cup Double in David Beckham's first full season in the first team.

For David it was a dream come true, perhaps almost unbelievable. He had just turned 21, and was already thought of highly. He was rated as a genuine prospect at international level, and had

THE BIG BREAKTHROUGH

turned out for England Under-21s team. In fact, while the country prepared for a summer of football with the European Championships – Euro 96 – being hosted by England, David went on holiday. But it would not take long for him to take the step up to the next level, and that process began on the very first day of the following season.

On 17 August 1996, at Selhurst Park, with Man United starting their defence of the Premiership title against Wimbledon, David scored what still must rank as one of his his most outrageous and probably most famous and celebrated goals. In the final minute of the game, with Man U leading 2–0, David collected the ball just inside his own half of the pitch. By his own account, he was just trying to achieve what teammate Jordi Cruyff had narrowly failed to do a few minutes earlier. In any case, he certainly succeeded. He spotted Wimbledon goalkeeper Neil Sullivan on the edge of his own penalty box, and lobbed him from inside his own half, about 55 yards from the goal. It went in.

And at that moment, David Beckham officially became famous.

4

Love at first sight

DAVID BECKHAM

LOVE AT FIRST SIGHT

When he became a regular in the first team David did a lot of growing up – and it did not all happen out on the pitch. This was a boy who had traded the comforts of his own family life for the family set-up at Old Trafford when he was about 16, and for the next four years he was happy enough to live in digs, mainly with Salford couple Annie and Tommy Kay.

But during his breakthrough season it became clear it was time for David to find his own place. So he bought his first bachelor pad – a brand new three-storey townhouse, in Worsley, North Manchester, just down the road from Ryan Giggs.

LOVE AT FIRST SIGHT

United's leftwinger had told Becks about the property when it came on the market, and once he moved in, the pair became closer friends.

Beckham was introduced into Ryan's circle – the Worsley Crew, as they were dubbed. They would regularly meet up for lunch at the local pub after training. Then at his place – not far from the United training ground – he had his own base, organised exactly as he wanted it, with a pool table and huge bedroom – where the TV popped out of a cabinet at the touch of a button.

David entertained his parents there when they visited from London and he probably entertained his girlfriends there too.

David's relationship with Deana had ended a while before, and he was now going out much more with his young teammates. As an increasingly well-known rising star at United, he met and then dated a procession of girls, such as Lisa Rys-Halska, a blonde air stewardess who later dated Ryan Giggs, and Julie Killelea, daughter of a wealthy United fan – who dated and then married Becks' teammate Philip Neville. Back in Essex there was model Leoni Marzell who later suggested David was as interested in talking to her dad about football as in her.

David was far more focused on his football

LOVE AT FIRST SIGHT

than on females – or, at least, the females he was meeting at the time. He was also clearly shy with the opposite sex, and one or two complained later that he barely spoke to them on dates. Former Miss UK Anna Bartley complained that David took her to a restaurant then said almost nothing to her. Clearly these were not relationships that set Becks' pulse racing. But that was about to change.

After the Double-winning season, and particularly after his goal at Wimbledon, it was only a matter of time before David gained full international honour. In Euro 96, England had progressed to the semi-final before being defeated by Germany in a penalty shoot-out (the second time they had done so in six years). Now, following the departure of Terry Venables, the national side had a new manager – Glenn Hoddle.

Hoddle was another hero of Beckham's – even though he was a Spurs rather than United legend. During the Eighties, Hoddle was the most gifted and creative midfielder in England, with fantastic vision and passing ability, and a scorer of some wonderful goals. There was a certain similarity between them, and it was soon clear that the admiration was mutual when Hoddle selected David for his first England squad. It was an away

LOVE AT FIRST SIGHT

game against Moldova – England's opening qualifying match for the 1998 World Cup Finals – and on 1 September (a date that would become very special for him as an England player) David Beckham won his first England cap in a 3–0 victory.

His next turnout for his country was significant for another reason. Because it was in Tiblisi, shortly before the Group 4 qualifier against Georgia, that David apparently first set eyes on Victoria Adams – Posh Spice.

It was in the run-up to the match, and David was relaxing in his hotel bedroom, watching a music video channel with Gary Neville, his friend, Man United teammate and now England roommate. As they watched, the video for the Spice Girls' new single *Say You'll Be There*, came on the screen. And there she was: Posh Spice, called Midnight Miss Suki in the video, pouting and strutting her stuff in skin-tight black PVC. David made his feelings at that moment quite clear. He told Gary: "That's the girl for me, and I'm going to get her."

That was quite a declaration, because although he was an increasingly high profile soccer player, she was a Spice Girl – a member of

LOVE AT FIRST SIGHT

the world's biggest pop act at that time. But, as it happened, within a few weeks events would conspire to bring David and Victoria together. In fact, fate had already taken a hand.

The Spice Girls were an overnight sensation in late 1996 and early '97. They had appeared apparently from nowhere to make number one with their first single, *Wannabe*. Their second single, *Say You'll Be There*, would do the same, with equally stratospheric sales as their first hit. They had captured the imagination of the public, particularly young girls, for their brand of feisty charm and individuality – not only in Britain, but all over the world.

In early '97 the Girls were being interviewed for a magazine and were shown pictures of current Premiership players, to see if there were any they liked the look of: Victoria picked out Manchester United's David Beckham. It was apparently the first time she had seen him, and she certainly liked what she saw.

So it was no coincidence that, a few weeks later, Victoria accompanied 'Sporty Spice' Melanie C and their manager, Man United fan Simon Fuller to see United play away at Chelsea for possibly the first match she had ever attended –

LOVE AT FIRST SIGHT

she knew absolutely nothing about football. After the game, in the player's lounge at Stamford Bridge, Victoria and David – Posh and Becks – met for the first time.

According to the man himself, what ensued was not exactly fireworks. When he was introduced to her by Fuller, David managed to mumble a 'hello' but was too tongue-tied to say much else – apparently he was too overwhelmed by seeing her in the flesh. He said later that he thought she was even more stunning than she looked on the telly.

But the following week, when Man United were playing at home to Sheffield Wednesday, she and Sporty turned up again with Fuller, and even went on the pitch at Old Trafford at half-time. This time, as some witnesses have noted, a spark of chemistry between them was definitely present when they met in the player's bar after the game.

It was real 'eyes meeting over a crowded room' stuff and Victoria, a little tipsy from drinking red wine, made a beeline for him. David, for his part, was not about to let his chance slip this time: he asked her out to dinner that night, and when she said she was busy, he made sure he got her phone number.

DAVID BECKHAM

LOVE AT FIRST SIGHT

It did not take him long to use it. He phoned her the very next day, and that evening they had their first date – a date that had more to do with their shared backgrounds rather than their lives as two stars in the parallel worlds of music and sport.

In fact they had a lot in common. Victoria came from Goff's Oak, about a 15-minute drive away from Chingford, where David grew up. Her family were certainly better off than the Beckhams: she lived in a big house with its own swimming pool, and her dad Tony drove a Rolls Royce. But then, he was a self-made man: he and wife Jackie, originally from Tottenham, North London, had a successful electrical wholesale business. In other words, Posh Spice was not really posh.

And in her way, Victoria was as single-minded, determined and focused on succeeding in her chosen field as David was in his. During her childhood and her teen years, while David had been dedicating all his energies to football, Victoria was doing the same with her all-abiding passion – show business. She sang, danced and performed from a young age and enrolled in an after-school stage school when she was eight. Like David she was following in parental footsteps – dad Tony had been in a pop group in the Sixties.

LOVE AT FIRST SIGHT

But while David sailed through his youth carried by his huge natural talent Victoria had experienced quite a difficult time. Despite her family's wealth, she still went to the local state school, and she found it hard to make friends. Her preoccupations with singing, dancing and all things theatrical did not necessarily enamour her to her classmates. In fact, some other girls made her life at school an absolute misery.

Like David, she found security, and the room to be herself, in the bosom of her family, with her mother, dad and younger siblings Louise and Christian. The Adams family, as David would find out, were (and remain) even more tight-knit than his own family.

Like many wanna-be actresses, Victoria auditioned time and time again but without success. Then she answered an ad in theatrical newspaper *The Stage* for members for a new girl-group. She auditioned successfully and was soon sharing digs and then a house with the other successful applicants: Geri Halliwell (whom she had already met at other auditions), Melanie Brown, Melanie Chisholm, and another girl never quite as dedicated as the others, who was later replaced by Emma Bunton. The Spice Girls had been formed.

DAVID BECKHAM

LOVE AT FIRST SIGHT

The bond that these girls established by living at such close quarters created the spirit that defined the Spice Girls, and Victoria held an important role among the five friends: she was considered very level-headeded, with business savvy. After two years of rehearsing and performing at the behest of the Spice Girls' original 'creators', it was Victoria who suggested that they break away and hook up with another management team who could further their ambitions more effectively. That is how under the guidance of Simon Fuller – later to create *Pop Idol* – the Spice Girls became international stars within a matter of months.

But when David took Victoria out that Sunday evening, they were like two ordinary young people from Essex. He met her outside a pub they both knew in Woodford in North East London, working out it was one of several places they had both frequented in the recent past. They drove around in his car for a while, deciding where to go, and eventually went to a Chinese restaurant for a drink. They were finally asked to leave because they did not want anything to eat. Then they went round to Mel C's house where they had a coffee and then Becks drove Posh back to her car.

It was a remarkably low-key evening for two

LOVE AT FIRST SIGHT

people who were already famous in their chosen fields, and who in a matter of weeks would together command the attention of the media as if they were royalty. David, shy as ever, had said little on that first date. The following morning Victoria went to America with the Spice Girls, but from that moment on they were in close contact via mobile phone. David found his communications problems melt away when talking to her on the phone, and their conversations would run into hours. As a result he started to run up some world class phone bills.

Things were initially complicated by the fact that Victoria did already have a boyfriend. In fact, she had actually been engaged, very briefly, to a previous one. But after that evening, she ended her relationship. Victoria and David began a relationship that, due to Victoria's vicious work commitments, consisted of a few stolen hours in Essex at Victoria's parents, Manchester, or anywhere else they could spend time together. But it was a relationship that quickly became like no other they had either experienced.

At first it was all supposed to be kept secret, but that just proved impossible. They were soon spotted out together and the press began to

LOVE AT FIRST SIGHT

speculate about a possible romance, and nothing that emanated from the couple or their families contradicted the rumours. In fact comments by Victoria and her mum Jackie made it perfectly clear that the Spice Girl was seeing plenty of young Mr Beckham. In fact both Posh and Becks clearly did not want to keep their relationship a secret – they were just too happy. They were falling – had already fallen – in love.

So in June '97 David went public with his relationship with Victoria. They were an item, he admitted. When they did not see each other, they spoke every day.

Not surprisingly this provoked a storm of media interest – just a foretaste of things to come. It immediately made Becks at least twice as famous as he already was – it put him on the front page, as opposed to the back page, of the newspapers for the first time.

And he was already pretty famous. Another stellar season with Man United had just ended. They had won the Premiership title again, this time at a canter, being proclaimed champions three weeks before the end of the season and running out winners by seven points. There had been some failures though – Man U did not win the FA Cup

LOVE AT FIRST SIGHT

and had failed to win the Champions League – but Becks' footballing reputation had greatly increased. Not only had he broken into the England team, but also in 1997 his fellow English professionals named him PFA Young Player Of The Year.

Skillful, energetic, a scorer of, but more particularly, a provider of goals, Beckham was regarded as a great talent and potentially a world-class player. His right foot was becoming recognised as a remarkable instrument – of pleasure for United and their supporters, or torture for their opponents. But now he was becoming renowned for more than his footballing prowess. He was now entering a different league: the world of celebrity.

Beckham's image would start to appear everywhere, and that in itself would affect his earning potential. He was already earning about £10,000 a week. Within months Becks had secured his first major endorsement deal with Brylcreem, worth around £1 million, which exploited what had already become obvious to millions: Becks was very interested in personal grooming, particularly the condition of his hair – still in its floppy-with-blonde-highlights phase.

But his relationship with Victoria had also

LOVE AT FIRST SIGHT

changed something else. Before he met her his focus on football, and to Manchester United in particular, was unswerving. Nothing was as important, nothing came between him and football. But after he met Victoria things clearly changed. He had found something that was, at least, a major distraction from the beautiful game.

Alex Ferguson was not slow to notice. After a summer of publicity about the Posh and Becks love match, 'the gaffer' made his own comment by sending David to play in a pre-season friendly at lowly Bournemouth. This happened the day before he should have turned out for the season's traditional big curtain raiser, the FA Charity Shield against Chelsea. The implication was that the tough Scotsman would not tolerate a slipping of the high standards that the player had set in the previous two seasons, and David, soon returned to the senior squad, was well aware of what was expected of him. However, the coming season was to prove to be a tough one.

It did not help that United skipper Roy Keane, who many considered the heart and the dynamo of the United team, was badly injured in October and missed the rest of the campaign. But

DAVID BECKHAM

LOVE AT FIRST SIGHT

David was now under a new kind of pressure – he began to face taunts from opposition fans about his new girlfriend. As the season progressed, they became increasingly obscene. He was understandably upset, and, in fact, he let it get to his game. He visibly reacted to the abuse of the particularly hostile supporters of West Ham. And he was now picking up as many yellow cards as goals because of his frequent losses of temper and rash tackles.

David's temperament was facing its first real test since he broke into United's first team, and it was a test made more difficult by the fact that having found his dream girl, her incredible workload meant that they spent a lot of time apart. He was actually quite lonely. In addition, because her fame was much greater than his, he was considered the junior partner in the relationship.

The truth was that they were two young people, 22 and 23-years-old, who were besotted with each other, and in late January 1998 came the announcement that had already been widely predicted for weeks. They had already decided to do it while she was in America, but Becks officially asked Victoria to marry him at a posh hotel in Cheshire. In the increasingly characteristic manner

LOVE AT FIRST SIGHT

of their affair it demonstrated David's evident thoughtfulness and romantic nature – and distinct lack of concern about splashing some serious cash.

Becks was already in the habit of sending Posh flowers wherever she was in the world. He filled their hotel room with roses and lilies before formally asking for her hand in marriage. She joyfully consented and they exchanged their rings: for her, a specially-designed £40,000 diamond ring, for him a diamond-studded gold band. It was just 10 months after they had first met.

That was the true start of Posh and Becks, a new team that was in some ways to rival to the other team in David's life, Man United. It would generate as much publicity, fascination, adoration and loathing, and considerable amounts of money. Perhaps from that moment David Beckham's departure from Manchester United was inevitable.

As it was, United ended the 1997–98 season without a trophy – the first time that had happened in several seasons. They lost the title to Arsenal who, just to rub it in, won the domestic Double. If it was David Beckham's first real taste of failure at United, there was a still a footballing bright side to the season and it came with England. Becks had played every game in the qualifying competition for World Cup '98 when England travelled to Rome for the final game against Italy in October '97 needing just a draw. England produced their best performance in years to draw 0–0, and snatch automatic qualification away from the Italians. Glenn Hoddle's England were on their way to the World Cup Finals in France.

So for most of that season David could look forward eagerly to playing in his first World Cup. Little was he to know that it could go so horribly wrong.

5

From disaster to triumph

DAVID BECKHAM

FROM DISASTER TO TRIUMPH

When the England squad arrived in France for World Cup 98, David Beckham had every reason to believe that he would be in the starting line-up when the team walked out for their first match against Tunisia in Marseilles. After all, he had played in every England qualifying game since breaking into the team nearly two years earlier.

But in the lead-up to the finals, things had not exactly gone well for the England set-up in general and for Becks in particular. England coach Glenn Hoddle had taken 27 players to their pre-tournament training camp in La Manga, Spain – but only a squad of 22 could go to the

FROM DISASTER TO TRIUMPH

World Cup. So on a very tense Sunday afternoon in early June, Hoddle informed the players individually whether or not they would be going to France. David was duly told he was in the final squad. But among those going home included his United teammates Phil Neville and Nicky Butt and, sensationally, Paul Gascoigne.

Hoddle believed that Gascoigne, although an inspirational player, might cause problems and decided not to take him. He ended Paul Gascoigne's England career in a hotel room in Spain. A distraught Gascoigne promptly trashed it.

David, with Gary Neville in a nearby room, apparently heard it all. It proved to be something of a bad omen, particularly for Becks. Hoddle's painful method of removing five players from the squad had created a difficult atmosphere among the remaining squad members, but also David's own relationship with the England coach was starting to fray.

Hoddle had already commented during the season on Becks' increasingly poor disciplinary record, and was certainly aware that his famous girlfriend, his own growing fame and fortune was setting him apart from the other England players. Then there was the behaviour that

FROM DISASTER TO TRIUMPH

seemed more in keeping with a pop star or a model than a professional footballer.

Like, for instance, wearing a sarong. Not long before the World Cup, David and Victoria had flown down to stay at Sir Elton John's mansion in the South of France, and when they were photographed on their way to a romantic dinner, David was wearing a Jean Paul Gaultier designed-sarong over his linen trousers. Not surprisingly this caused a range of reactions back home from outrage to amusement to intrigue.

Beckham had suffered the abuse of football supporters all over the country the previous season and had experienced other, more frightening evidence of the dark side of fame. David had received hate mail and even bullets through the post to his home in Worsley. But Posh and Becks were not about to be deterred. Their life was nobody's business but their own – even if they clearly revelled in much of the attention they received.

So when Hoddle gave the squad some time off prior to the opening game, not surprisingly David chose to spend it with his fiancée – who had flown to Spain especially – rather than play golf with his squad mates. This did not go down well with the coach, and was not helped by Becks' tepid display

FROM DISASTER TO TRIUMPH

in a warm-up game against a local team.

Hoddle announced his team for the Tunisia game to the squad two days before the match: the name 'Beckham' did not feature in the starting eleven. David, although he probably already sensed Hoddle's displeasure, was devastated. Hoddle would delay publicly announcing the team until just before kick-off, but to make matters worse, before then he forced Becks to face the press in the daily press conference knowing he was out of the team. His forlorn demeanour immediately had the assembled journalists speculating that Beckham had been dropped.

It was a form of humiliation visited on the player by the manager, who when confronted by Becks about his decision, informed him he did not think him sufficiently focused – clearly suggesting that his relationship with Posh Spice was affecting his football. This made David even more upset, and he made little effort to hide his feelings.

With England winning their opening match against Tunisia 2–0 David was unlikely to be recalled for the next game against Romania, and duly stayed on the sub's bench. But with England 1–0 down, he was sent on as substitute in the second half, together with 17-year-old Michael

DAVID BECKHAM

FROM DISASTER TO TRIUMPH

Owen, to taste his first World Cup action. He soon set up England's equaliser, scored by Owen.

But England still ended up losing that game 2–1. It meant that to progress to the knockout stage of the competition, they almost certainly had to win their final group game against Colombia. But after his contribution in the Romania game, Hoddle could not seriously consider leaving Beckham out of the team again. So he played, and David responded, like he has responded to his critics and doubters many times since, in the best way possible.

England were already 1–0 up when they were awarded a free kick 25 yards from the Colombia goal, in a central position. Beckham whipped the ball over the defensive wall of four Colombian players and beyond the goalkeeper's right hand into the corner of the net. It was a trademark Beckham goal. And it meant that England would progress to the last 16 of the World Cup – to play Argentina.

This was a huge match, due to the respective positions of both countries in world football, and the particular rivalry between the sides, created by previous World Cup meetings in 1966 and 1986. In between these games, in 1982, had been the altogether more serious matter of the Falklands War between the two countries.

DAVID BECKHAM

FROM DISASTER TO TRIUMPH

That night in Saint-Etienne proved to be no less explosive, but it was also a match that came to haunt David Beckham. 1–0 down after less than ten minutes – a penalty, given away by keeper David Seaman – England had rallied to go 2–1 ahead, with a penalty of their own, and a goal by Michael Owen that ranked with Maradona's second against England 12 years earlier. Becks played a clever pass which saw the teenage prodigy run from the halfway line, cutting through the Argentinian defence like a hot knife through butter, and score brilliantly. But Argentina equalised, with a clever free kick, just before half-time to make the score 2–2.

England were in a fight, but had a great chance, particularly with Owen and Beckham playing. But what happened next is probably David Beckham's lowest moment in football. Just after half-time the fearsome Argentinian midfielder Diego Simeone scythed him down from behind. It was a bad foul, and Simeone followed up by ruffling Beckham's hair. And then Beckham reacted, petulantly kicking out against Simeone – who himself hit the deck as if poleaxed. Danish referee Kim Neilson's action, egged on by several Argentinian players, was

FROM DISASTER TO TRIUMPH

immediate and unforgiving: he gave David the red card. Becks had been sent off. Becks saw the red card, turned around and walked the few short yards to the tunnel without looking anywhere, certainly at the England bench and a scowling Glenn Hoddle.

With only 10 men and still 40 minutes to go, England hung on. Then Sol Campbell, up for a corner, headed the ball in the Argentina net. But the goal was disallowed. The goal went into extra time and then penalties.

It had been a great achievement by England to reach this far, but it was to end there. Without Beckham on the pitch, England had to rely on non-spot kick specialists like David Batty and Paul Ince to take penalties, both of whom missed. England were beaten and on their way home.

David Beckham had sat through the rest of the game in the dressing room. He then apologised to his teammates, some of whom were not in a very forgiving mood. Centre half Tony Adams was more consoling and sat with him for a while. Hoddle said absolutely nothing to him. That was just the start of a very difficult period for Becks.

The judgement on England's defeat by the British press, and the country at large, was

FROM DISASTER TO TRIUMPH

immediate and final: it was all Beckham's fault. The initial reaction was perhaps understandable, but the consequences were excessive, ghoulish, and frightening, especially when further whipped up by the tabloids – *the Daily Mirror* ran a dartboard with Becks face as the bullseye.

This was most famously symbolised by the effigy of Beckham which was hung from a lamppost outside a pub in South London after the game, but somehow even worse was the fact that David's parents became the targets of vile abuse at their home in Chingford.

David's immediate reaction did not necessarily help. Having returned to England with the squad he immediately flew to New York, to be with Victoria, who was in the middle of a big American concert tour with the Spice Girls. Apart from simply needing to get away from the gathering storm around him, he needed to be near Victoria because she had told him, just before the Argentina game, that she was pregnant with their first child.

He was overjoyed at the news of becoming a father for the first time. In fact it was this fact that consoled David and strengthened him in his fast-developing new attitude – there was more to life than football.

DAVID BECKHAM

FROM DISASTER TO TRIUMPH

But many people did not share this view. During the next few weeks he stayed at Victoria's side as the Spice Girls toured across America.

But on returning to Britain in July he was confronted with the full force of his new reputation as public enemy number one. He had to be given a police escort at Heathrow Airport, and police protection for some time thereafter. It was not safe for him to live in Worsley on his own, so his mum and dad were advised to stay with him.

There was even talk about Man United having to sell Beckham – it was the first time that his name was linked with the likes of Real Madrid. But Alex Ferguson was having none of it. He made sure that David was occupied by looking ahead to playing football and nothing else. And David's commitment to United was demonstrated when he signed a new five-year contract before the season started, worth £6 million.

Beckham's strength of character started to resurface. At United's first away game of the season at West Ham United he faced a barrage of abuse from first whistle to last, but came through the test with undamaged resolve. He almost took strength from the taunts, putting in superlative performances for United as they progressed at

FROM DISASTER TO TRIUMPH

home and in Europe, and the abuse finally subsided. It was clearly time to move on from England's World Cup exit.

David and Victoria were never out of the papers, or magazines. After Victoria's pregnancy was announced, far from withdrawing from public gaze, she proudly and justifiably displayed her growing bump at numerous showbiz events, and at photo shoots. The couple appeared at a fashion show at London Fashion Week in the autumn and were virtually mobbed. By Christmas, Becks' football career was back on track, and he had just added a lucrative sponsorship deal with Pepsi. At the beginning of 1999 he bought himself a Ferrari, costing £150,000.

Posh and Becks were a new kind of royalty: they were rich, beautiful, clued-up, but still identifiably ordinary, and millions of people – not only from England, but all over the world – were fascinated with them. Victoria was happily talking about raising the baby in a decidedly unposh way – without the help of a nanny – despite their full and pressurised working lives. David just talked about how much he was looking forward to becoming a dad.

Then on 4 March 1999 Victoria was taken to

FROM DISASTER TO TRIUMPH

the Portland Hospital in central London, where she gave birth, by caesarean section, to a 7lb boy. In the manner of a royal birth, an overjoyed Becks went outside the hospital to inform the world's press that mother and baby were well and he was "over the moon."

His name was Brooklyn Joseph Beckham – Brooklyn for the New York borough where Victoria was staying when she discovered she was pregnant and told David. Victoria spent several days recuperating in a private room in the hospital and a besotted Becks also often slept in the room with mother and baby. Then they left the hospital by limousine with police escort in a presidential-style getaway.

It was nine months since the events of the World Cup, and things could not have been better. He had even faced his adversary Simeone again in the Champions League for United against Inter Milan in the Champions League, and had his revenge in a 2–0 victory at Old Trafford. From despair he was joyful at the birth of his son, and the prospect of marrying his sweetheart in a few months time. And things were hotting up for a tremendous climax to the season for Manchester United.

DAVID BECKHAM

FROM DISASTER TO TRIUMPH

United were still fighting on three fronts: the Premiership, the FA Cup and the Champions League. In the Premiership it was nip and tuck with Arsenal, the reigning champions, who just had their noses in front. Then Man U met Arsenal in the FA Cup semi-finals, a tie that went to a replay. That game was to shape the rest of United's season, although Becks' own contribution was overshadowed by those of his teammates, goalkeeper Peter Schmeichel and Ryan Giggs.

David opened the scoring in the Villa Park replay with a tremendous shot from outside the penalty area, but Arsenal equalised. Late in the game United skipper Roy Keane was sent off, and then, in the final minute of the game, the Gunners were awarded a penalty. If penalty-taker Dennis Bergkamp scored United were beaten, but Schmeichel saved it.

That set up 30 minutes of extra time in which 10-man United continually repelled the full-strength Arsenal. But then Ryan Giggs picked up a misplaced pass in his own half and started running towards the Arsenal goal. A few seconds later, having rounded several defenders, he smashed the ball past Gunners' goalie David Seaman, scoring one of the great goals in the long

FROM DISASTER TO TRIUMPH

history of the FA Cup in one of it's best ever games. United won 2–1. A famous victory was greeted with euphoria from United fans.

The following Wednesday they travelled to Italy to play Juventus in the second leg of the Champions League semi-final, having disappointingly drawn 1–1 at Old Trafford two weeks previously. Within 10 minutes United were 2–0 down and seemingly out of it. But Roy Keane scored an inspirational header from a corner by Becks, and by half-time they had equalised. They scored again in the second half for a famous comeback 3–2 victory. As well as contesting an FA Cup Final, United were now in the Champions League final – and chasing an unprecedented, historic Treble.

The first part was achieved when United won the Premiership on the final day of the league season. They had to beat Spurs at Old Trafford to be sure of the title, and they did so, coming from behind to win 2–1, with Becks scoring the equaliser. Then United completed their third Double in five years – and David's second – when they comfortably beat Newcastle United 2–0 in the FA Cup Final.

Just four days later they were in Barcelona to play Bayern Munich in the Champions League Final. As everyone in football knew, this was the

FROM DISASTER TO TRIUMPH

moment of truth for Alex Ferguson, who had long seen the European trophy as his Holy Grail, the one trophy that had so far eluded his grasp.

And it was the occasion when Ferguson chose to place David Beckham in the position he longed to play in, but so rarely did – central midfield.

Ferguson had always believed that Becks' best position was wide on the right of midfield and there was no question he was one of the most dangerous players in the world in that position. But 'the gaffer's' hand was forced by the suspension of Roy Keane. Beckham had wanted to prove himself in the more important central position and was getting his opportunity in the biggest game possible.

Things did not go well – Bayern went ahead in the first half, and were in control with several opportunities to increase their lead. But United rode their luck and more importantly, their attitude and energy and belief, epitomised by Beckham, never faded. Finally, as the game passed the 90 minutes mark that attitude found its reward.

United forced a corner on the left. Beckham took it, it was cleared to Ryan Giggs, who shot and Teddy Sheringham, just on as a substitute, redirected the ball into the corner of the net. United had equalised in injury time. 1-1 and

FROM DISASTER TO TRIUMPH

everyone thought the game would go into extra time. But United won another corner on the left: Becks took it again, Sheringham headed his cross goalwards and Ole Gunnar Solskjaer, United's other sub, hooked the ball into the roof of the net.

Seconds later, the final whistle went. Manchester United were European Champions and they had won an unprecedented Treble. David Beckham had won his biggest honour yet in club football, and he was just about to claim what he considered his biggest prize of all.

6

The coronation of Posh and Becks

DAVID BECKHAM

A CORONATION OF POSH AND BECKS

I t had been a momentous 12 months for Becks. It was a year that had seen the complete resurrection of his footballing reputation after the disaster of France 98. He had knuckled down, rediscovered his discipline, blanked out the abuse, and produced great performances time and again on the way to the ultimate reward – United's historic Treble.

It was a year that had seen a big leap in his wealth. As well as becoming among United's top earning players – about £20,000 a week by this stage – he was securing lucrative sponsorship deal after sponsorship deal: a multi-million pound deal

A CORONATION OF POSH AND BECKS

with Pepsi had recently followed his seven-year, £4 million deal with Adidas. He was named by *France Football Magazine* as the second highest paid footballer in the world after Brazilian superstar Ronaldo – earning around £3 million a year.

Posh and Becks were now virtually a national institution – just like the Royals, yet more popular. Every event they attended was likely to make the front pages of the tabloids. They could hardly be ignored, as they had taken to appearing in public in matching outfits, like the matching leather suits they wore to the Gucci party in June. They were bigger than any other celebrity couple of the time, and becoming the fascination of an international audience. David in particular was becoming known for his acts of thoughtfulness and romantic nature, as revealed by Posh, like his constant love notes to her and his tendency to visit her when she least expected it.

But to some observers it seemed that it was hardly possible that the perfect couple could be so perfectly in love. After all, they seemed to be courting publicity almost as much as they courted each other. These observers would also assume, by dint of her greater wealth and more forceful personality, that Victoria was the driving force in the relationship.

DAVID BECKHAM

A CORONATION OF POSH AND BECKS

Becks and Posh soon realised that the media and their coverage in it was something that could be, in fact had to be, carefully managed. Their dealings with the media were certainly a lot more successful than the Royals. In public David Beckham has always appeared comfortable and confident. A commanding presence, but not overbearingly so. And he invariably looks great, wearing the pick of the styles from his and Posh's favourite designers like Prada, Versace and Gucci. Fashion was certainly one reason why Posh and Becks were soulmates. They could indulge their shared obsession of clothes and jewellery, as they demonstrated with numerous and increasingly lavish tokens of love.

But David was clearly not just into fashionable clothes; he was a trendsetter. When he wore that Gaultier sarong before the '98 World Cup they immediately sold out. He had chosen the Versace suits that the Man United team had worn in Barcelona before and after their biggest match in 30 years, the Champions League Final. He had true style and was being recognised for it – readers of *GQ Magazine* made him their most stylish man of the year, for the first but certainly not the last time, in 1999.

DAVID BECKHAM

A CORONATION OF POSH AND BECKS

Posh and Becks' wedding was planned like a major royal occasion. It took over a year of meticulous organisation by Victoria herself and her mother Jackie, with the invaluable help of Peregrine Armstrong-Jones, who was certainly a man with a royal pedigree – he was the brother of Lord Snowden, ex-husband to the Queen's sister Princess Margaret.

And the wedding was themed as a fairy tale union of a prince and princess – a sort of Walt Disney version of a royal romance. Complete with a coat-of-arms that famously adorned the wedding invitations – and had heraldry experts up in arms – their own flag containing the initials 'VDB' flying from above an image of the castle in Ireland where they were to be married, and matching his-and-her thrones.

Although the wedding was a bit of fun, it was also a major event, organised with military precision – and a very lucrative exercise for the soon-to-be Mr and Mrs Beckham. Posh and Becks sold the exclusive photo and interview rights to the wedding to *OK!* magazine for a cool £1 million.

On 4 July 1999, nearly 300 guests arrived at the castle, including most of the United team – (but not Alex Ferguson, who was attending

David Beckham's first game for England was in 1996 against Moldova. He has been a regular team member since. In November 2000 he was first made captain of the side for a game against Italy.

David Beckham is probably the most famous man in Britain and probably the most popular. Not only is he England's leading footballer, but also a family man and iconic figure around the world.

Victoria and David Beckham married in 1999 and have two children, Brooklyn and Romeo.

The Beckham's first public appearance in London, April 2004 following 'revelations' in the press about David. The glamourous couple were attending a party for their management company, and displayed open affection for each other as they faced the press and photographers.

A CORONATION OF POSH AND BECKS

another wedding), the Spice Girls (but not the departed Geri Halliwell) and a good few more celebrities (although Sir Elton John was struck down with illness and could not make it). The nature of the deal with *OK!* meant that security was extremely tight, which served a useful purpose of keeping out all undesirables from the occasion – but particularly photographers from rival publications posing as guests.

It was an absolutely beautiful day. The castle rooms were adorned with ivy and fresh apples in a Robin Hood style. An 18-piece orchestra welcomed the guests, later entertaining them with versions of Spice Girls hits. Most of the guests stayed in the main hall while the Bishop of Cork conducted the marriage service before a small congregation of family and friends. It took place in a chapel-like folly in the grounds, which had been specially blessed by the Church of Ireland.

Becks was wearing a Timothy Everett cream suit, as he waited for his bride, with best man Gary Neville at his side and four-month old Brooklyn in his arms.

At around 4.30pm the bride appeared on the arm of her father, wearing a £60,000 Vera Wang wedding dress – she described it later as "very

A CORONATION OF POSH AND BECKS

Scarlett O'Hara" – a diamond and gold coronet and, underneath, a corset by Mr Pearl.

It was a very emotional occasion and tears flowed, not least by David himself. The Bishop told the congregation there was a lot of interest in the marriage, "but what matters is what is in David's heart and what is in Victoria's." They exchanged rings; both designed by Asprey & Garrard – a diamond ring set in 18-carat gold for her, a diamond and gold eternity ring for him. When they were pronounced man and wife the congregation whooped and cheered. The bride and groom and the immediate friends and family then joined the other guests in a Robin-Hood-themed marquee in the grounds of the castle to celebrate the marriage with pink champagne. And like royalty, David and Victoria (and Brooklyn) sat apart from their guests in a private alcove.

Then, after the wedding dinner, the speeches began: father of the bride Tony Adams came first, welcoming David into the family – "We know we couldn't wish for a better son-in-law" he said – followed by David himself. His near opening line of "My wife and I" was cheered to the rafters. Then, according to tradition, he profusely thanked his new parents-in-law, as well as Victoria's brother

A CORONATION OF POSH AND BECKS

Christian and sister Louise.

Then came the best man's speech from Becks' best friend and teammate Gary Neville who, although apparently extremely nervous beforehand, performed the task in his usual capable fashion, and told a few good jokes into the bargain. He said he had a telegram from Diego Simeone, then held up a red card. As well as a genuine telegram of congratulations from Alex Ferguson there were also messages "from Prada, Gucci, Tiffany, British Telecom and Ferrari – best wishes and thanks for your support."

Then the party began in earnest in a second Moroccan-style marquee, and as the evening progressed, the new Mr and Mrs Beckham slipped off. But far from leaving their party early for a honeymoon destination, they returned in matching purple attire – another play on the royal theme. The festivities ended with a spectacular firework display, but the evening was not yet over for David and Victoria – they still had to select the very special wedding photos that would appear a few days later in *OK!*

Not surprisingly the sheer grandeur and ostentation of the occasion came in for more criticism, as well as fascination. Although it laid

A CORONATION OF POSH AND BECKS

the template for the future successful TV series *Footballers Wives*, much of the 'royal' trappings were clearly tongue-in-cheek. There was also a nice sense of proportion about their wedding present choices: they asked their guests either for vouchers from Marks & Spencer and Selfridges or to make a donation to the Meningitis Trust – the charity that Victoria had supported since Brooklyn's birth.

Alex Ferguson believed that the role of a footballer's wife was to support her husband, so instead of granting Becks' a special dispensation to enjoy a 10-day honeymoon in the Indian Ocean, Ferguson chose to enforce the allotted start date for Becks' pre-season training. David and Victoria stole a few days, their first as a married couple, in the South of France before Becks had to return. He soon found himself turning out for Man United reserves against non-leaguers Selby Town. Ferguson had certainly made his point: nothing was more important than Manchester United. Becks had been brought down to earth before the coming season with a bump. But it did nothing to improve Ferguson's relationship with the player – or his wife.

Things were to get much worse. Ironically the trigger for the breakdown in relations

A CORONATION OF POSH AND BECKS

between Becks and his manager and mentor was the thing that Ferguson had hoped would lead to David and Victoria leading a more settled life: the arrival of Brooklyn.

But with the excitement came the anxieties and pressures that all new parents face, seemingly magnified several times over due to their considerable fame. In many ways it became more difficult because Posh and Becks were determined to be decidedly un-royal-like with the new baby, but an ordinary modern couple. Before his birth Victoria had spoken confidently in interviews about them raising Brooklyn themselves without the help of a nanny, and the baby becoming seamlessly incorporated into her busy schedule with the Spice Girls. But as nearly all new mothers discover once the baby arrives, the reality is quite different.

The enormity of bringing a new life into the world struck Victoria immediately after the birth. One of the first things she said to Becks, as he held his newborn son, was: "Whatever you do, please don't leave him." David hardly needed to be told, he was overcome with emotion, and keenly felt the weight of responsibility. He fretted over the baby with almost the same intensity as Victoria, and readily took on the usual run of the mill and

A CORONATION OF POSH AND BECKS

exhausting duties of a new parent: changing nappies and administering feeds – at all times of day or night.

In fact, a sort of reversal of the usual roles of the sexes was already in place when it came to their home life. David was almost notoriously neat and tidy – Posh later called him "an obsessive compulsive" about keeping an orderly house – while Victoria was a self-confessed hater of housework. So perhaps the arrival of Brooklyn was in some ways an easier transition for Becks than it was for Posh.

Earlier in the year Posh and Becks had (finally) moved into their luxury apartment in Alderley Edge, Cheshire – a move that was particularly welcomed by Ferguson. Now Beckham and his new family would be based near Manchester permanently – or so he hoped.

But after Brooklyn's birth Posh and Becks headed directly to her parents' home in Goff's Oak, and in the subsequent months it was clear that Posh was still spending much of her time there, not in Cheshire. That was hardly surprising in the circumstances. She needed her family's support more than ever, added to the fact that her sister Louise had herself recently given birth to a daughter. Needless to say her work and social contacts were all based in or around London.

But this hardly made things easier for Becks regarding his club. In the months after his birth, Becks was often driving long distances, sometimes late at night, just to be with Victoria and Brooklyn for a few hours – and this was during United's draining assault on winning three different trophies.

Brooklyn had the usual range of ailments that affect young infants, including having trouble keeping down food – he actually threw up over his dad's wedding suit before the marriage ceremony – and Victoria had confessed to being a "paranoid" mother, always fretting about the infant's health. A more serious episode occurred when it was discovered after a few months that Brooklyn had an umbilic hernia, and had to return to hospital to have it corrected.

It was a non life-threatening routine procedure, but a distressing moment nonetheless for his parents – especially Victoria.

But a far more serious issue was coming into focus, the one of security. In October 1999, the police informed Posh and Becks about a possible plot to kidnap Brooklyn. David was on England duty at the time, preparing for a home game against

A CORONATION OF POSH AND BECKS

Luxembourg in the latter stages of qualifying for Euro 2000. Victoria was in Goff's Oak, and understandably became frantic.

David and Victoria had been aware of the dark side of fame since France 98 and even before that. They had received abusive and threatening mail on a regular basis almost as soon as their relationship began and had also been stalked most recently by a woman who sat in the grounds of their Alderley Edge home and finally had to be sectioned by the Mental Health Act.

By this point England had a new manager, Kevin Keegan, an inspirational player in his time, a former European Player of the Year, and a successful manager at both Newcastle United and Fulham. Keegan had taken over, originally as a temporary appointment, when the FA fired Glenn Hoddle in early '99. Keegan was clearly far more understanding about the trappings of success and fame than his predecessor, and above all appreciated that for Becks, his family came first.

Keegan organised for Victoria and Brooklyn to stay at the England hotel for the rest of that night, even though it was just before the important match. It was a sensible decision, which allayed a worried mother's fears – at least for now. But it

A CORONATION OF POSH AND BECKS

was followed, some weeks later, by an alleged incident as the family left Harrods in London after a shopping expedition. According to Posh and Becks, someone apparently made a lunge for Brooklyn, although there was confusion as to what actually had occurred.

David and Victoria's concern about the baby led to the unfortunate circumstances of David's sister Lynne's wedding, also in late '99. Brooklyn was apparently ill once more, so David attended the wedding without Victoria or Brooklyn – a huge disappointment for the Beckham family who longed for their grandson to be present. Thankfully it was nothing serious – but that only further encouraged speculation about the state of relations between Victoria and her in-laws.

The truth was that there had been a shift because David had found the love of his life and his first priority was now Victoria and their child – while Victoria needed them, plus her own family. It was certainly not her style to fit in with David's family, or his friends. At another wedding in December, between Becks' teammate Philip Neville and Julie Killelea – who dated Becks briefly before falling for Phil – women guests were requested to wear red, white and black, the Manchester United colours. Posh felt unable to comply, arriving instead in a stunning coffee-coloured gown which, some tabloids noted, rather upstaged the bride's wedding frock.

Clearly between Brooklyn's birth and the wedding four months later Posh had been working on her figure to look fantastic for her big day, and she had succeeded magnificently. After the wedding if anything she appeared to get thinner. She was reportedly now a size 6. When she became a catwalk model for a fashion show during London Fashion Week in early 2000 she was positively waif-like. There was much speculation in the papers that the extraordinary change in her physique was the result of some kind of eating disorder. Posh and her people, including her mother Jackie, strongly denied it.

By this stage there was no point Alex Ferguson even bothering to pretend that the Beckham family unit had settled firmly and permanently in the north west of England. In some ways it was surprising that Becks managed to avoid a real bust-up with 'the gaffer' before it actually happened. But United's excellent form clearly helped: they had continued on from the Treble season with a more than satisfactory start to their

A CORONATION OF POSH AND BECKS

defence of the Premiership title in 1999–2000, and were progressing well in the Champions League.

But Becks did finally overstep the mark when he openly flouted club rules before a Champions League away game in Austria. Man U were due to fly out to play Sturm Graz and Ferguson put his players on a club curfew the night before the game. But Becks broke it – he accompanied Victoria to a party hosted by Jade Jagger. When he found out, Ferguson refrained from publicly commenting, but it was discovered later that he reacted by fining Becks two weeks wages – around £50,000.

Was this a sign of Becks getting too big for his boots again? It was not the only fine he received around that time, although it was what came with it that really hurt: an £800 fine for speeding was accompanied by an eight-month driving ban. For a man who loved driving fast cars – by this time his collection included a Ferrari 550 Maranello, and an Aston Martin DB7 – and was obviously still driving up and down motorways between Manchester and London on a very regular basis – this was disastrous.

Luckily for Becks the driving ban proved to be temporary. His immediate appeal against the ban was successful – although again shrouded in controversy. Rather unusually the appeal judge accepted his "celebrity defence" – that he was speeding near his Alderley Edge home because he was being tailed by a paparazzi photographer. After the alleged incident in Harrods a short time before the appeal, and with certain echoes of the manner of Princess Diana's death two years earlier, Becks' story just seemed to sum up (to the judge at least) the pressures the Beckhams were now under.

But, a short while later when Beckham came up with a feasible excuse for missing a training session, Ferguson chose to be far less forgiving.

7

How Becks became captain of England

DAVID BECKHAM

HOW BECKS BECAME CAPTAIN OF ENGLAND

Sniping comments about failings in Becks' character on a football pitch had certainly faded since the World Cup in '98. His tremendous performances since then, particularly in the Champions League, were honoured at the end of 1999 when he claimed second place in the European Player Of The Year award, narrowly beaten to the title by Brazilian forward Rivaldo. But in early 2000 Becks was sent off for the first time as a Manchester United player for a high tackle in a game against Mexican side Necaxa in the World Club Championship in Rio de Janeiro.

The Rio trip became like an unofficial midseason break for Becks because he was suspended for the next game and United was soon eliminated from the tournament anyway. And he managed to achieve another long-held ambition by playing football with the kids on Rio's famous Copacabana Beach. But he was about to receive a rude awakening from this blissful episode.

Back in England in mid-February, Becks was with his wife and 11-month-old baby in Essex, and about to return to Manchester for training the next day. But Brooklyn had been quite badly ill during the day and worse in the evening, leading Becks to delay driving north until the following morning. The fretful father rose early to set off still seriously concerned about his infant son, who the doctor had eventually diagnosed as having gastro-enteritis. So concerned, in fact, that having travelled a few miles up the motorway he turned back.

Becks then phoned Steve McLaren, Ferguson's deputy, leaving a message that he would be missing morning training because of Brooklyn's condition – but neglecting to mention that he was near London rather than near Manchester. When Brooklyn awoke it was clear he was much improved so Becks set off again, but by this point he had missed training. When he arrived the following morning,

HOW BECKS BECAME CAPTAIN OF ENGLAND

all hell broke loose.

Perhaps it would have helped if David had spoken to the boss and explained the situation before the training session began, but he did not. As a result Ferguson very publicly singled out Becks in the middle of training, ordering him to spend the rest of the session with the reserves (a huge insult to the pride of a first team regular).

Afterwards the manager and the player had a heated argument. It was clear that Fergie was not satisfied with Becks' stated reason for skipping training, a feeling fuelled by seeing pictures in the morning paper of Victoria attending the British Fashion Awards the previous evening. Ferguson apparently used the word "gallivanting" to describe Posh's behaviour, and Becks, not surprisingly sprung to her defence. He also made it clear to 'the gaffer' that he did not like the insinuation that he was babysitting Brooklyn while his wife was out partying.

Ferguson responded to this insubordination by dropping Beckham from the team for the next game at Leeds United – then United's nearest challengers for the title – and dishing out his second £50,000 fine in a matter of months. He was not even named as a substitute. By the following day the story was in the papers and at the match there were almost as many cameras trained at Becks watching from the stands, as there were on the match itself (which United won, 1–0).

The major bust-up with Ferguson had, in truth, been a while coming. But it was still a shock for Becks when it finally arrived, particularly to be suddenly excluded from the first-team set-up. If nothing else it was a salutary reminder that United was a huge part of his life, and that, as a kid, to play football for United was all he ever wanted to do. Also he could not afford to take things for granted at a club which set its standards so highly.

So he was very pleased to 'kiss and make up' with Fergie and be restored to the first team a week or so later. He made a statement declaring his wholehearted commitment to the United, but the incident did have a disconcerting end, which said a lot about the underlying tensions that now existed between the men.

David's considerable playing ability was not the only reason why Posh (and Tony Stephens, his agent) lobbied for him to be United's top paid player. Man United was the biggest, most profitable football club in the world, with not just a British but worldwide following, particularly in Asia. And Becks' marketing value to United was

HOW BECKS BECAME CAPTAIN OF ENGLAND

clearly huge. He was worth a fortune to the club in terms of the number of replica shirts that were sold with his name on the back alone. Ted Beckham and his son may have been Cockney Reds. Now David Beckham was a big reason why there were Bangkok Reds or Shanghai Reds.

So by mid-2000 Becks' pay-packet at United had rapidly swelled to around £60,000 a week, and it would continue to rise as leading foreign clubs like AC Milan and Barcelona made overtures to hire his services.

His last contract with United, signed in 2002, which gave him earnings of around £90,000 a week, was delayed for a long time precisely over the question of 'image rights.'

Maybe it's just as well that soon after the big bust-up with Fergie, Becks presented to the world a serious image change. Later he would experiment with having a variety of styles, from the Mohican to cornrows, but it was the first radical haircut that caused the biggest sensation when he famously replaced his trademark boyish floppy locks with a number two skinhead cut that cost £300.

He went from being the Brylcreem Boy – and fairly soon afterwards his relationship with one of his first sponsors ended – to looking like United's

HOW BECKS BECAME CAPTAIN OF ENGLAND

shaven-headed hardman Roy Keane's more sensitive younger brother. Naturally it made the front pages – and even the comment pages – of the newspapers. Some regarded it as a statement of intent by a new Beckham, the reformed character, who intended to change his celebrity ways.

Although he had made his peace with 'the gaffer', Becks was clearly not about to adopt a low profile – it was certainly not on Posh's agenda. The couple were interviewed for the Rolls Royce of celebrity magazines *Vanity Fair*, and photographed by the world's leading celebrity snapper Annie Liebowitz in a mansion in the Scottish highlands. Then Brooklyn's first birthday prompted a major celebration in a Cheshire hotel where several of the United players and their children were invited.

By this time, United were cruising to their latest Premiership title. Becks, like his fellow Class of '92 members, would shortly be sporting his fourth Championship winners medal. Football experts readily agreed that this was an awesome United team. But they were not so successful this time in Europe.

They met Real Madrid in the quarter finals of the Champions League, and although they drew 0–0 at the Bernabau, a stunning passage of play by

HOW BECKS BECAME CAPTAIN OF ENGLAND

the Spanish side – who had yet to sign the likes of Ronaldo, Figo and Zidane – put them 3–0 up at Old Trafford. United staged a late comeback in vain, including a stunning Beckham goal where he dribbled past several players, including future teammate Roberto Carlos, and smashed the ball high into the net. United were out of Europe, but there was still more European football for Becks and several other United players to look forward to.

Under Kevin Keegan, England had scraped into the finals of Euro 2000 (hosted by both Holland and Belgium) via the play-offs, where they played Scotland, won 2–0 at Hampden Park, then lost 1–0 in their last game against the old enemy at Wembley. It proved to be a disappointing tournament for England, but ironically it proved a heartening watershed for Becks.

As is so often the case, things had to get worse before they got better. England played Portugal in their first group game and started brilliantly, rushing into a 2–0 lead, with both goals set up by Beckham crosses from the right. But Portugal immediately pulled one back (a wonderful shot by future teammate Luis Figo) and it was 2–2 by halftime. Portugal scored the winner in the second half, and as the disconsolate England players left the field, Becks became the object of abuse by a group of England 'fans'. Their tirade involved not only the usual vile comments about Victoria but also Brooklyn. An angry Beckham responded with an upraised finger to the group. At the same time, Victoria who attended the game with her father, was jostled by jeering supporters. It was a nightmare scenario for Becks, who was always extremely protective of Posh's well being at games.

Becks' upraised finger not surprisingly made the following morning's papers, and provoked some predictable outrage, but as it turned out this was no repeat of St. Etienne. For a start, Kevin Keegan had heard the hideous abuse David had received and solidly supported his player. An upsurge of revulsion against the so-called fans and sympathy for Becks (and Posh) soon followed. In their next match, the crucial clash against Germany, Becks was greeted at the warm-up before the game with a new sound: England fans singing, "There's only one David Beckham." It was a significant moment in Becks' England career, soon to be followed by another.

England won the Germany game 1–0 and Becks once again set up the goal, scored by skipper Alan Shearer. It was England's first victory

HOW BECKS BECAME CAPTAIN OF ENGLAND

against the Germans in a competitive match since the World Cup Final in 1966. It was also a dire, dour game, and although England were back in the tournament it proved to be a false dawn. In the next match they lost to Romania 3–2.

In fact, England were just not very good – a team largely in transition who would soon lose their mainstays of the previous few years like Shearer and Tony Adams. However, David's reputation was enhanced once more – among commentators as well as England fans. He was recognised, with the likes of Michael Owen, as the cream of the next generation. And it was nearly time for that generation to take over.

By the following September, Keegan's reign as England manager was over, finishing in miserable fashion, as England once more played Germany, in the first qualifying match for the next World Cup. It was the national side's final game at Wembley, their famous old home, before it was due to be knocked down and rebuilt.

England lost 1–0 with a terrible performance unfit to grace the old stadium. Keegan, too nice a man to be insensitive to criticism, decided there and then it was time to leave, and told his shocked players in the changing room after the match. Becks

HOW BECKS BECAME CAPTAIN OF ENGLAND

was particularly upset as he valued Keegan as a friend as well as a coach. But his departure possibly hastened the next major step in his own career.

Having drawn the next qualifier in Finland, temporary control of the national side was handed to Leicester City boss Peter Taylor for the friendly fixture against Italy in Turin. This was to be an inexperienced and fairly experimental England team, and with the international retirement of Shearer a new captain was needed. To the astonishment of many, Taylor appointed David Beckham for the job.

It was a shock choice for several reasons. Becks had never even skippered Man United, and unlike, say, his friend Gary Neville, he was not known for shouting out instructions or encouragement to his teammates on the pitch. The captaincy was usually the preserve of solid defenders like Neville rather than fair players like Beckham.

But this so far temporary appointment said a lot about Beckham's new standing with England supporters and also in international football generally – he was soon to be voted into second place as World Footballer Of The Year. It was also for one game only.

So what leadership qualities did Becks

HOW BECKS BECAME CAPTAIN OF ENGLAND

actually possess? The world, and to some extent the man himself, was about to find out.

England lost that game in Italy, but it was a positive performance from a young England team. Beckham's awareness of his new responsibility was evident when he did not react to several provocative challenges from Italian players. He was taking his new role seriously and he was also sending out a message to the incoming, permanent England manager to give him the job long-term.

It turned out that the man appointed to the job, controversial as his appointment was, sensibly saw that David Beckham played a crucial role in the creation of the new England set-up. Sven Goran-Eriksson, who became the first non-English England manager in history, did not have much time to turn things round. England were near the bottom of their qualifying group with a single point. There was little margin for error.

Eriksson's appointment caused a storm of protest from within the English game, but it marked a sea-change for the national side, and there was general approval when he confirmed Becks as England captain for his first match in charge, a friendly against Spain.

It proved to be an easy victory and although

DAVID BECKHAM

HOW BECKS BECAME CAPTAIN OF ENGLAND

Becks only played the first half he acquitted himself well enough. Clearly the England skipper's job was now his – less than three years after his red card against Argentina had made such an outcome absolutely laughable. And it made a very satisfactory addition to the two latest acquisitions in Becks' life: a £1 million deal with 'Police' sunglasses, and a £185,000 Lamborghini Diablo GT.

All of a sudden things were very different for England. This was now a national side who, with no permanent 'home ground', would be playing their home matches at stadia all over the country – the grounds of England's leading club sides. This in itself helped create a different atmosphere. Eriksson's first competitive game was against Finland at Anfield, home of Liverpool – and where Man United players could usually expect to receive a hostile reception. He was soon experiencing the enormous pressure that comes with the England job – England were soon losing 1–0 (a Gary Neville own goal).

Fortunately Michael Owen grabbed an equaliser just before half-time. Then early in the second half Becks scored what turned out to be the winner – coming in on the right to shoot in the far

HOW BECKS BECAME CAPTAIN OF ENGLAND

corner, his first goal for his country from open play. England goalie David Seaman made a brilliant save near the end to preserve the lead, and England's World Cup qualifying campaign was up and running. And Becks had given a captain's performance. Even at Anfield the crowd were not slow to show their appreciation.

Becks' England captaincy also said something about modern Britain. By now he was an icon of the age in a way that transcended football. He was all things to all people, even to those who weren't interested in the 'beautiful game'. The main basis for this adoration was Beckham's good looks, his fashion sense and style, allied to what people saw as a down-to-earth niceness and a very English ability not to take himself too seriously. He was an icon to all – to the gay population and to the black population, because he clearly embraced aspects of black culture, particularly music.

Posh and Becks were also on personal terms with some of the biggest designers in the fashion world, including Donatella Versace and 'Dolce E Gabbana'. And his graduation as a fashion icon was confirmed when he became the first sportsman to grace the cover of *The Face* magazine in the

HOW BECKS BECAME CAPTAIN OF ENGLAND

summer of 2001, controversially photographed as if his head had been dipped in blood (it was actually soy sauce). Some would find it hard to believe that this was the captain of the England football team. It was a long way from the days of Bobby Moore and 1966.

By the summer of 2001 United had won yet another title in their usual steamroller fashion. This was Becks' fifth championship victory, and in the latter stages of the season he had celebrated his 200th appearance for United – a stunning 6–1 victory over their strongest rivals Arsenal. As it turned out, it was the penultimate winners medal he would win as a United player.

But as the 2001–02 season got under way, there was the more pressing matter of a World Cup qualifier in Germany...

8

The Lionheart

DAVID BECKHAM

THE LIONHEART

On 1 September 2001 – five years to the day since his England debut – David Beckham led out the England team at the Olympic Stadium in Munich for the crunch match in World Cup qualifying group 9 against Germany. It was the third, meeting between these two giants of world football, and two great rivals, in the past 15 months.

Each country had registered a victory in the previous two clashes. But the Germans had by far the better record over a longer period, and had been responsible for eliminating England from World Cups and European Championships

THE LIONHEART

on several occasions since 1966 – ask any long-suffering England fan.

Although Germany were strong favourites for automatic qualification for World Cup 20002 in Japan and Korea, England approached the game without the huge weight of expectancy that usually accompanies the national side's big matches. The press certainly seemed convinced that a win against Germany on their own turf was a pretty far-fetched idea. At the same time the new-look England side under Sven Goran-Eriksson was starting to show some promising form in qualifying games. They had recently beaten Greece, Albania and Mexico and Becks had scored four goals since becoming captain of the side.

But coming into the Germany game Becks was actually suffering from one of his very rare injuries – a groin injury – and for much of the week it was touch-and-go whether he would play or not. His absence would have undoubtedly been a huge blow to the England team – and a massive morale booster for the opposition. Because, as Eriksson clearly understood, Beckham now was the player that other national teams respected and feared most. He symbolised England to the outside world.

Becks was passed fit to play, albeit wearing

protective cycling shorts, and on that Saturday evening in Munich he led out a quietly confident England side – who promptly went behind to an early German goal. Things looked bleak, but from that point on, everything started to go right for the England team. For a start, Beckham swiftly removed the cycling shorts and immediately felt freer to move. Then a quick equaliser by Michael Owen and a goal by Steven Gerrard on the stroke of half-time made it 2–1 to England.

2–1 became 3–1 just after the break, with another goal by Owen, who then completed his hat trick a few minutes later. With 20 minutes still to go Emile Heskey thumped in the fifth goal and England ran out 5–1 winners. By the end the England team were toying with their opponents.

It was an incredible result, something that finally laid the ghost of numerous previous defeats against the Germans. Because of the margin of victory, it also now completely turned around the fortunes of the respective nations in the qualifying group. Now England were in the box seat, and consequently the pressure was on them to achieve automatic qualification for the World Cup Finals. The pressure was immediately apparent, as England made much harder work of

THE LIONHEART

beating Albania at home, a few days after the Munich game.

But in October 2001, in their final round of games of Group 9, England just needed to win at home against Greece to qualify for the 2002 World Cup – or do no worse than Germany, who were playing Finland at home at the same time. And it was at this moment where David Beckham enjoyed what many believe to be his finest hour on a football pitch.

Maybe it was destined to happen. The game was being played at Old Trafford, his home ground, and it was the first time that Becks would skipper a side there. England were also playing in an unusual all-white strip specially for the occasion – Becks always loved to play in all white, his favourite Man U away strip – and the colours the great Real Madrid.

Victoria, who had recently revealed on the *Parkinson* TV chat show – when both she and Becks appeared together and she sang a song from her first album – that her nickname for her husband was 'Goldenballs', could not be there because she was working in Italy.

In the tunnel before the game he also met the England mascot for the day, a tiny girl named

THE LIONHEART

Kirsty Howard. Kirsty's dignity and positive disposition in the face of her terrible disabilities – she was born with her heart the wrong way round and other organs in the wrong places – made an immediate impression on Becks. It was the beginning of a friendship with the terminally ill youngster who was on her way to raising over £1 million for charity, and she proved to be an inspiration to the England skipper.

While his teammates apparently racked with nerves and playing awfully, Beckham increasingly shouldered the responsibility for the whole team. By the second half, with England 1–0 down, Becks seemed to be everywhere on the pitch at once – tackling, passing, driving his underperforming teammates on. Finally, England equalised, and naturally he was involved as Teddy Sheringham headed in Beckham's free kick. But Greece almost immediately scored again.

Now it felt like Becks was taking them all on his own. England won a series of free kicks, all within range of Beckham's phenomenal combination of power and accuracy, but it was the one part of his game that was failing him. Until, with the game well beyond the 90th minute, England won yet another free kick in

THE LIONHEART

range of the Greek goal. Teddy Sheringham, who won the free kick, wanted to take it, but his skipper overruled him for one last effort.

This time there was no mistake. Beckham hit a soaring, wickedly bending shot into the top left corner of the goal that the keeper barely saw, let alone came close to stopping. The score became 2–2. The final whistle went a few seconds later. And then came the news from Germany that they had drawn 0–0 with Finland. It meant England had qualified for the World Cup in the most dramatic circumstances possible. The stadium and the whole country were electrified.

That moment encapsulated pretty much everything about David Beckham: not only the great skill to do something extraordinary, but the temperament of a truly world class player to produce the goods under the most extreme pressure. As one football commentator said at the time: "With players like David Beckham you feel there are certain moments of destiny...." suggesting the level of expectation that surrounded Becks at that moment. Then he delivered.

It also showed once and for all that Becks was more than just a flair player, a fancy dan: the

THE LIONHEART

tremendous fitness and workrate that he put into his performances, often overlooked by critics, could never be overlooked again. But there was also the sense of drama – the destiny as the commentator described it – as if the Gods smiled upon him. After all, if the Germans had won their game against Finland, the free kick would have meant nothing. As it was, it meant everything. No wonder Posh had dubbed him 'Goldenballs'.

As for England supporters, Becks' redemption from the fiasco of France 98 was complete. He had won English hearts once and for all, and even the Germans, who had been crushed again, could not help but admire him.

At the end of the year Becks could add the BBC Sports Personality Of The Year to his list of accolades, the overwhelming choice of the voting public, and almost entirely as a result of that free kick against Greece. Shortly afterwards he was runner-up for FIFA World Player Of The Year for the second time. Then there were the non-sporting accolades: *Heat* Magazine's Best Dressed Man Of The Year followed by *GQ's* Best Dressed Man Of The Year.

Early in 2002 Becks would announce he was taking up fashion designing – helping Marks &

THE LIONHEART

Spencer design a range of Beckham-branded boys clothes, a deal worth between £1 and £2 million. And the Beckhams would shortly make it into the movies – sort of. Certainly Becks' most famous talent – the one he expressed so well against Greece – was being immortalised: *Bend It Like Beckham*, a low-budget British film, whose main character was a most unusual footballer – an Indian girl from a strict Sikh family. It would become a big hit in the UK, and later would find even greater success in the US. Posh and Becks had also reportedly been interested in playing themselves in the film's final airport scene, but ultimately were played by body doubles, because their schedules did not permit it.

Posh was certainly very busy with her solo career, although this had hardly run smoothly following the break-up of the Spice Girls the year before. Her debut solo single *Out Of Your Mind*, a collaboration with Truesteppers and Dane Bowers, narrowly failed to reach number one in August 2000, in an almighty scrap for the top spot with Spiller's Groovejet (featuring Sophie Ellis-Baxter on vocals).

By late 2001, while her hubby was leading his country on a victory charge, she was busy

THE LIONHEART

promoting that album. On the *Parkinson* show, she sang *IOU*, which she had written for David, and became almost tearful. Becks responded by telling Parky that it was not really his type of music, but "her album has actually made it into my car" – not exactly the most gracious thing he could have said. But then again, Posh never professed to know anything about football.

Meanwhile, while Becks' England lionhearts were flying, things were looking quite different for the team who paid the lion's share of his wages. 2001–02 would pan out to be a strange and ultimately painful one for Manchester United. And it would effectively mark the beginning of the end of David Beckham's career with the club.

It had begun billed as Alex Ferguson's last season as manager – he was due to retire at the end of the campaign and it was by no means certain what was going to happen when he left. Who would take over? Would Fergie still have a role at United? Speculation filled the newspaper back pages for months. Furthermore, Sir Alex's highly regarded number two Steve McClaren (who also performed the same role for Sven Goran-Eriksson at international level) had left before the season began to become manager at

THE LIONHEART

Middlesbrough, so Fergie no longer had an assistant. Changes in the side had seen the arrival of Ruud van Nistelroy in attack and Juan Sebastian Veron in midfield, at an outlay of £50m, but also the sudden departure of lynchpin defender Jaap Stam.

As the new year began United found themselves in the unusually low position of fifth place in the league – and Becks had hardly played in the first team for weeks. First of all, if he had delighted the English with his heroics against Greece, he had not similarly impressed his tough Scots club manager. Fergie's only remark to Becks when he returned to the club was: "I hope you're going to work bloody hard now you're back at United."

In fact Becks did look below par following his almost superhuman exertions against Greece, so Fergie dropped him for most of the games as they approached Christmas. This was also set against the backdrop of Beckham's contract negotiations with United. They had now been dragging on for almost a year and were reaching a critical stage – the club knew if they did not have an agreement with David soon, he would be within his rights to sign a pre-contract agreement with another club. He could then

THE LIONHEART

leave United after another season and the club would not receive a penny in transfer fees.

Then in February 2002 Sir Alex suddenly announced that he had changed his mind about retiring. Ironically, considering his poor opinion of Posh's influence over Becks, it was reported his own wife had persuaded him to stay on. Immediately this had a beneficial effect on the team and their improved form in the second half of the season would have given United a record fourth successive title had the frontrunners Arsenal repeated their last minute stumble of the previous season and cracked. But this time they did not. In fact they won the title at Old Trafford by beating United 1–0. Arsenal went on to win the FA Cup, thereby doing the elusive Double – United were knocked out in an earlier round, ironically enough, by Steve McClaren's Middlesbrough.

The Red Devils' misery was complete, and furthermore Becks had missed the final run-in to the season. But this time his absence was the result of an injury – possibly the most publicised football injury in history.

By March 2002, United were looking more like their best in the Champions League, where they met Spanish side Deportivo La Coruna in the

THE LIONHEART

quarter finals. Having lost twice to Deportivo in the first group stages of the competition, they won impressively 2–0 in Spain in the first leg with an in-form Becks scoring a 30-yard wonder goal. It was the highlight of his best ever season of goalscoring in a United shirt, with 16 goals in both the Premiership and Champions League that season. Towards the end of that match Becks was badly fouled which left him travelling away from the match on crutches. His ankle was just badly bruised, not broken, as he had first feared.

But there would be no such luck in the return fixture at Old Trafford. About 20 minutes into the match Becks went into a challenge with a Deportivo player, which once again left him writhing in agony. And this time there was no doubt: he had broken a small bone, called the second metatarsal, in his left foot. The broken metatarsal, would become the focus of near-frenzied debate in Britain for weeks to come.

It was just a few weeks until England played in their first game of the World Cup Finals. Would they have to play without their most influential player and talismanic captain, or could Becks' left foot heal in time? The nation's concern for Becks' injury was anguished, but also

THE LIONHEART

touched with moments of comedy: *The Sun* newspaper printed put the injured left foot on its front page, asking its readers for a "laying of hands" to make it better. And as Becks is so heavily right-footed one wag inevitably remarked "I didn't know he had a left foot."

It was a race against time – and of course it was not just a question of the metatarsal healing, it was also a question of Becks' match fitness. Man U's season ended on a low note when they were beaten in the Champions League by German side Bayer Leverkusen. David had been unable to play a part at the season's climax and made it onto the pitch just once. In the final home match of the season, after 18 months of wheeling and dealing, Becks signed his new contract in the centre circle before kick-off in front of 65,000 people – a three year £15 million deal, worth around £90,000 a week.

Fergie embraced him on the pitch. For a minute, it was just like old times. But ultimately, Becks' signature on his last United contract was worth around £20 million for United.

By this point the prognosis on the metatarsal injury was good. Under the supervision of United's excellent physiotherapists, he did gym work at United's training ground Carrington and

THE LIONHEART

swimming in his own pool at Beckingham Palace – his rehabilitation therapy was relentless. It was a big relief to Eriksson who believed Becks was so important to the team that if he had been unfit he would have taken him along anyway as a non-playing captain.

Becks has publicly wondered whether what happened next was the decisive moment in his future departure from Man United. Before their departure to the Far East, the England squad were to travel to Dubai for a week of post-season rest, recuperation and light training, together with their families. Although he knew that Ferguson would have preferred him to continue his recovery treatment back at United, Becks decided to join the England party in Dubai, with Posh – now almost six months pregnant with their second child – and Brooklyn. For a week he worked with England's staff of physios, then it was off to Japan.

It was crunch time. Becks was driving his car two weeks after the foot was broken – and immediately had a car crash where thankfully no further injury occurred – and running by mid-May, but now he had to join in proper training sessions with the England squad to see if the injury would stand up. He took the plunge and survived. He was going to make it. It was a very proud David Beckham who led out England in Saitama on 2 June against Sweden. His first game in a World Cup Finals since that miserable night in St Etienne four years earlier, and now he was skippering the national team.

He and the team certainly started well enough and after 23 minutes a Beckham corner was headed in by Sol Campbell. But England's performance quickly deteriorated after that, their drive and purpose seeming to drain away, and Sweden deservedly equalised early in the second half. By this point Becks was tiring badly and was substituted. It was hardly surprising that he was struggling – it was his first game since the fateful Deportivo match in April.

The game ended 1–1 with the England side looking decidedly jaded. It was not the start they wanted, or needed – their next match was against none other than the famous rivals and tournament favourites Argentina. They had just won their first game. This was now a massive match for England – a game they really had to win to prevent an early exit from the World Cup.

It was time for another massive moment in the David Beckham story.

9

End of an era

DAVID BECKHAM

END OF AN ERA

Wherever they travelled in Japan – and they had to play each of their first round games in different venues – the England players were bowled over by the welcome they received from the local people. They were greeted by cheering crowds of men, women, children, and even old ladies, in England shirts. It was as if the Japanese people had adopted England as their team for the tournament – even though as host nation they were represented themselves.

Of course the main reason for this enthusiasm was David Beckham. Becks is a superstar in Japan, even though this is a country where the people have no tradition in the sport of soccer. The combined forces of television and advertising had already made him a popular figure in a culture which has long been fascinated with Western icons, and the coming World Cup greatly accelerated the Japanese obsession with Be-Ka-Mu – as he is known there.

Despite his obvious exhaustion in the Sweden game – Becks was actually somewhat annoyed at being subbed – his injured left foot had held up. He was up for it, and so were the team, and this latest meeting of England and Argentina, undoubtedly one of the biggest fixtures in world football – this one being played in the state-of-the-art Sapporo stadium under a roof – was to be just as electrifying as the previous encounters. And just a bit special for Mr Beckham.

England were fired up from the start, then fired up further by a bad foul on England defender Ashley Cole by Argentina striker Gabriel Batistuta in the first minute. They took the game to Argentina, controlling the game largely due to a commanding performance by Becks' United teammate Nicky Butt. Michael Owen went close, hitting a post. Then, in the last minute of the half Becks was fouled in the build-up to another England attack. Referee Collina

END OF AN ERA

waved play-on, because England still had the ball. Owen went round an Argentina defender in the penalty box then went over. Penalty.

Who would take it? Owen was probably the first choice, but then Becks was grabbing the ball off him. He was taking it.

Somehow no one expected it, and no one had really foreseen it. Millions of people on the other side of the world had gathered in pubs, public squares or simply to watch at home – a whole country that had more or less ground to a halt on that weekday lunchtime to watch this epic contest collectively held its breath. Could this really be happening? Everyone knew Becks took free kicks. Did he take penalties? He had certainly never taken one for England before.

He lined up to take it – but he could not. None other than Diego Simeone was standing in front of the ball, with the referee trying to move him away. This was now pure theatre. He went to shake Becks' hand, Becks was having none of it. On the other side of the world a nation growled its approval. Now he would have his moment. Right foot, the ball straight down the middle as the goalkeeper fell to his right. Pandemonium.

In the second half, England did not sit back

as they had against Sweden. Instead they set about Argentina again, and could have easily added to their lead. But in the last twenty minutes it was all one way traffic with the Argentinians laying siege to the England goal, the England team pushed further back as they manfully defended their lead.

Becks was looking tired again, but this time he refused to be substituted. He had to be out there with the team – his team. Some brilliant defending by Sol Campbell and Rio Ferdinand, and some superb goalkeeping by David Seaman and England were home and dry. Final score: 1–0 to England. Scorer: Beckham. England had done it. They had laid another ghost to rest. They had beaten Argentina for the first time in the World Cup since 1966.

And, of course, Becks had done it. The hurt over the game against Argentina four years earlier had finally been laid to rest. The England supporters had, in truth, already forgiven him for that. But now, he could finally end the personal torment over the events in St Etienne for good.

England were now going to qualify for the next stage of the tournament – so long as they did not mess up their next game against Nigeria.

END OF AN ERA

Played in stifling heat and humidity, they managed the minimum, playing out a 0–0 bore draw which left the players – particularly Becks, drained for hours afterwards. Unfortunately it also meant that if they were to beat their next opponents Denmark they would probably play Brazil.

The Danes, who had previously overcome the world champions France, greatly helped England by partly self-destructing during the first 45 minutes. A goalkeeping error led to England's first goal after a Becks corner, and by half-time England were leading 3–0 and won by the same scoreline. They were beginning to look impressive, and, crucially, Becks was looking fitter with every game. Unfortunately he came out of the Denmark match feeling far more pain in his left foot than in the previous ones, because the wet conditions had forced him to change his boots. And this was perhaps crucial in the outcome of the next game, which was to be the real test. Because as expected the next game, the quarter-finals, would see England meet Brazil.

It rained the day before the game, but on the day of the match it was sunny and hot. Conditions to suit the irrepressible, supremely talented but ominously well-organised Brazilians.

DAVID BECKHAM

END OF AN ERA

England started solidly and went ahead, with Michael Owen coolly profiting from Brazilian defender Lucio's mistake. 1–0 to England. Things were looking good as the half drew to a close, when Brazil equalised – the consequence of a Beckham misjudgement, which might well have been affected by his injury. As he was letting the ball run out of play to claim a throw-in, Brazilian leftback and Becks long-time adversary Roberto Carlos came into challenge for the ball and Becks jumped up. The ball did not cross the line; Roberto Carlos kept it in. Seconds later the ball was with Rivaldo and he was stroking the ball past David Seaman for Brazil's equaliser.

Already deflated by conceding a goal just before half-time, England then conceded another just after half-time in bizarre circumstances: Ronaldihno's free kick catching Seaman unawares and creeping under the crossbar. Everyone watching believed that the Brazilian would cross the ball from the kick, and no one could tell whether the 'shot' was deliberate or just a mishit fluke. The outcome, however, was all that was important. Even though Ronaldihno would be sent-off shortly afterwards, reducing Brazil to 10 men, England could not muster a decent response.

DAVID BECKHAM

END OF AN ERA

It was a sad, rather limp way to go, but England's World Cup dream was over. And Brazil would go on to win the trophy for the fifth time – beating Germany in the final.

David returned home to the now-heavily-pregnant Posh and Brooklyn, to prepare for the coming season and the birth of their second child. He had not seen them for over a month, because although the other players' wives flew out to Japan for a few days after the Denmark game, Posh, due to her condition, was advised not to fly. He also returned to the latest addition to his collection of fantastic cars, a new £165,000 Bentley – a 27th birthday present from Victoria.

Even if Becks' life was a now a series of dramatic incidents, there was barely a sign of the events of the months to come.

On 1 September – exactly a year after England's 5–1 victory in Munich – Victoria gave birth to her and David's second child, again in the private Portland Hospital in London: a healthy baby boy, named Romeo.

There was inevitably much speculation about the choice of the baby's name, but needless to say, Becks was soon requesting his boot sponsors Adidas to send him football boots with his new

END OF AN ERA

son's name stitched into the tongues, and he would shortly be adding to his range of tattoos.

By this point the new season had begun and for the first time in a while Becks was playing for Manchester United. The fans were no doubt happy that he, only partially fit for England in the summer, would be reaching proper fitness for their (and his) beloved club. Sir Alex certainly appeared to be – he made Becks skipper for a series of league matches and for a Champions League game for the first time at the end of September. It was almost 10 years exactly since his first ever appearance for the first team as a raw 17-year-old at Brighton.

It was a temporary appointment while club skipper Roy Keane was out of the team but it appeared that Becks had surprised Fergie with his leadership qualities for England. The United boss said so publicly, while also making more pointed remarks about how the player should focus on his football with United. It was, of course, the same issue that he had bothered Fergie ever since a pop star named Victoria Adams came into Becks life in 1997. After the birth of Brooklyn it had led to an almighty row between player and manager that had been settled, but never quite been forgotten. Now, after the birth of Romeo, it would lead to

END OF AN ERA

another confrontation, another breach, which would never be forgotten or forgiven.

In November a Sunday newspaper revealed another kidnap plot targeted at the Beckhams. This time, the paper claimed the aim was to snatch Victoria, Brooklyn and the baby. Four men and a woman were arrested for conspiracy after reporters had infiltrated an alleged kidnappers' ring. It would lead a few months later to a court case in which the charges against the accused would be dropped. But the effect of the new scare at the time was to establish a heightened level of security in terms of personnel and equipment around the Beckhams at all times.

Fergie gave Becks some time off as a result of the kidnap scare, but not before he turned out in a Worthington Cup tie against Leicester City and incurred another injury – a broken rib. He then joined up with the England team for a get together and went to visit the Queen at Buckingham Palace for the second time. The he went to Barbados for a week with his family,

In his latest autobiography *My Side*, published later in 2003, Becks describes how Fergie's attitude to him had distinctly cooled after he returned from his break. In fact, he claims that

END OF AN ERA

for the next three months his life was made a misery at United, particularly on the training ground at Carrington. When he confronted 'the gaffer' about it, he discovered that his meeting-up with the England squad and going to the Palace, instead of recuperating from his rib injury, was what particularly irked Fergie.

The fact was the whole England business probably irked Fergie, and a lot of Man United supporters besides. Because as well as having to contend with the influence of Posh, Sir Alex was now perfectly aware that England coach Sven Goran-Eriksson had a closer relationship with Becks than he did.

Furthermore many of the Old Trafford faithful were aware that Becks' performances for United, in the last two seasons, had not regularly reached the old commanding heights. Becks has admitted himself that he was off his game in the early part of the season. And if he was being frozen out at United, as he imagined, he would discover that when it came to the crunch the United fans would not weep over his departure.

Although they went on to win their seventh league title in nine seasons, David's future with the club was the matter of almost daily speculation in

END OF AN ERA

the media, and it had everything to do with what happened on 15 February 2003, the day of the notorious 'flying boot' incident.

On that day United lost 2–0 to Arsenal at Old Trafford, in the FA Cup, and memories of Arsenal's Premiership-winning victory at Old Trafford the previous season were painfully revived.

Afterwards in the dressing room an angry Ferguson allegedly blamed Beckham for his part in one of the Gunners' goals. Becks objected to being singled out for criticism over how the goal was conceded. This just infuriated the manager further, and during the ensuing argument he kicked a football boot in the player's direction. It flew up and hit Becks in the face, just above the left eye, causing a cut. Becks lost it. He flew at Ferguson, and had to be restrained by his teammates.

Things would never be the same. The incident soon reached the outside world, and despite Ferguson's almost immediate apology and statements on both sides attempting to defuse the situation – Becks was clearly furious. No one was left in any doubt what had happened, because the next day Becks let at least one photographer take a shot of the bandaged cut – the evidence of Fergie's temper.

END OF AN ERA

Rumours of Becks' departure from Old Trafford to any number of foreign clubs soon followed. Inter Milan were mentioned but Real Madrid soon emerged as firm favourites to sign him. For his part Becks laughed off the speculation. In fact he did nothing to improve his chances of a move to the giant Spanish club, when he played in United's match against Real at the Bernabau in the Champions League quarter final first leg in early April. In a devastating 3–1 defeat for United Becks was particularly disappointing – although it transpired he was carrying a hamstring injury for most of the game.

But the rumours continued, and became stronger. There were extremely conflicting signals coming out of Madrid, the team who had signed a world superstar footballer every year for the previous three seasons: Figo, Zidane then Ronaldo. Real's club president Florentino Perez had released a statement that Madrid would "never" buy Beckham. "We have no intention of negotiating a transfer."

But everyone knew that this was exactly the same tactics that the wily Perez had used to lure Ronaldo to Real the previous season. The statements coming out of the Beckham camp were

END OF AN ERA

not exactly discouraging either. "Any player would be honoured to be spoken about by Real Madrid," Becks reportedly stated. Meanwhile Posh was seen nodding when asked at a party if she was planning to move to a new country soon.

In the return game of the United-Madrid quarter-final at Old Trafford, Becks looked on from the subs bench for an hour, then came on when United were losing and scored two goals – one a brilliant free kick – as United rallied to win 4–3 on the night. It was an emotional moment for Becks. After half the Real team had attempted to swap shirts with him, he went to all four corners of Old Trafford to commune with the United fans. If it was not a farewell gesture, it was a very good impression of one.

A few weeks later he had played his last game for United at Old Trafford against Charlton in a 4–1 win and scored.

A few days later Becks played his final game for Manchester United at Everton. He scored from another wonderful free kick. He lifted the Premiership trophy as a United player for the sixth and final time.

After that, the race to sign David Beckham was on, and there was only likely to be one winner.

10

The Becks a man can get

DAVID BECKHAM

THE BECKS A MAN CAN GET

B y the time of Becks' move to Madrid, Mrs Beckham was working hard on the relaunch of her singing career.

Posh was looking for a new start, and a new sound. She found it in an area of music that was more to her husband's taste hip-hop and R&B. As a result she started collaborating with the multi-millionaire American hip-hop producer/entrepreneur Damon Dash. As the 2002–03 football season was drawing to its climax – and the rumours of Becks departure from Man United were reaching fever pitch – Posh was quite often in New York, working for her new album with Dash.

DAVID BECKHAM

THE BECKS A MAN CAN GET

It is interesting to speculate how Becks felt about this development. Shy, soft-spoken and courteous though he is, Becks was also furiously protective of his wife, and had shown both on the pitch and against Fergie that he could show his temper when the issue of Posh was involved. He also admitted, in his autobiography *My Side*, released shortly after his arrival at Real Madrid, that he was in a state of depression following the World Cup, which made life difficult for Victoria. The treatment that he believed that Fergie was giving him following his rib injury in November made matters worse.

On top of everything, Becks was also having to absorb the fact that his parents Ted and Sandra had divorced after more than 30 years of marriage. This was clearly something he found difficult to deal with and to talk about openly to both his parents, and it was also clear that a rift had developed between David and his father.

Ted, who had put his son's football before everything and had fulfilled a dream when David became a Manchester United player, was distraught that he might actually leave the club. "I shall tell him not to go," he had told an interviewer, a public display of his feelings that clearly upset

THE BECKS A MAN CAN GET

and angered Becks. It led to a serious parting of the ways between the father and son.

Becks was still close to his mum Sandra, and she was clearly very concerned about her son. In a revealing moment in *My Side*, Becks' revealed that about this time Sandra had actually confronted Fergie about his treatment of David. Beckham picks out one part of Fergie's response to his mother as significant: "Do you know Sandra, the trouble with David is that everybody sucks up to him now."

Now his wife was often away, with a music producer who had a fairly notorious reputation as a womaniser. And Posh and Dash were clearly hitting it off, as it was soon announced that Posh would be modelling for his fashion label Rocowear.

After travelling to South Africa with the England squad, Becks was soon back with Posh. They made a trip to the United States, where they discovered that Man United were indeed prepared to sell him. A short while later, on 17 June, Becks' agent Tony Stephens phoned him to say that the deal with Real Madrid was done.

On 2 July, David Beckham signed on the dotted line and officially became a Real Madrid player. At a press conference attended by 600 members of the world's media he was welcomed

THE BECKS A MAN CAN GET

with a speech by Real president Florentino Perez. He made a very short speech himself (including words in Spanish) and the legendary Real player Alfredo di Stefano presented Becks with his shirt.

On the back of the shirt were his name and his allotted squad number for the coming season: 23. Seven, the number he wore for Man United and England was already taken by Raul, the undisputed prince of the great Madrid club. With his customary charm, Becks had brushed aside the issue: of course seven was Raul's number. Instead Posh reminded him that 23 was the number worn by his favourite ever sports star, the basketball player Michael Jordan.

Everybody knew that the number 23 shirt was worth a fortune to Real Madrid. On the basis of Manchester United's merchandising revenues, particularly on shirts with Beckham on the back, it was clear that the merchandising and marketing advantages of having Becks as a Real Madrid player were massive. In the next few months they were going to sell an awful lot of Beckham shirts.

All eyes were on Becks once more. Could he cut the mustard in a team with more world class talent than possibly any side in history – Ronaldo, Zidane, Figo, Roberto Carlos, and Raul? Was he actually good enough to be a galactico? The Spanish media were sceptical. As for the Real fans, it had taken them a long time to truly embrace both Ronaldo and Zidane, generally considered the best two players on earth, so what were the Englishman's chances?

Many wondered where he would actually play in the team. His long-held position at United was wide right of midfield, but that was Luis Figo's position at Real. However, the team's new coach was none other than Carlos Queiroz, formerly number two to Alex Ferguson, and he had plans for Becks: he would play at the heart of the team in central midfield. So Becks was actually fulfilling yet another dream – playing for Real Madrid and playing in his favourite position, the one so long denied him by Fergie.

It was a new challenge, and once more he delivered. After looking unexceptional in pre-season games, Beckham was nothing short of a phenomenon once the Spanish season started properly.

It was not only his pinpoint crosses and his fantastic free kicks; it was his tremendous energy, stamina, and teamwork. He was actually the perfect compliment to a team of stars: a star who left his ego in the changing room. "Beyond the ad campaigns, the dyed hair, the changes of look, the premature autobiography and the famous singing wife, Beckham is making it plain that he is also a quite fabulous football player," purred *Marca*, the Madrid sports paper.

At the same time, he was busy leading England into another major football tournament: Euro 2004. After the World Cup, and England's rather limp performance against Brazil, the English press had their knives unsheathed and were ready to tear into Sven Goran-Eriksson, given half the chance. Following a scrappy victory in Slovakia, England had drawn at home 2–2 with unfancied Macedonia in the Euro 2004 qualifying campaign – Becks scored in both games – then lost badly in a friendly against Australia where Eriksson played two completely different teams in each half. The press were preparing to pounce when England met their main opponents in the group Turkey – a very strong side that had made the semi-finals at the 2002 World Cup.

In an excellent performance England won 2–0 at the Stadium Of Light in Sunderland – Becks scored again, a late penalty – but crowd trouble and anti-Turkish chanting marred the game.

England met Turkey in Istanbul in the final

THE BECKS A MAN CAN GET

group match in October 2003. England fans were banned from attending the game due to the first match in Sunderland, and the history of violence when English supporters travelled to Turkey. England needed just a draw to qualify, but if they lost it would mean going into the play-offs. The atmosphere for the game could not have possibly been more hostile. As usual Becks was at the centre of things.

Firstly he missed a penalty in bizarre circumstances. Slipping as he went to kick the ball, the ball not only ballooned over the bar, it almost cleared the stadium. Becks even smiled after it happened, but was soon involved with Turkish defender Alpay, both after the penalty miss and at half-time, which led to a major fracas between several players from both sides. As in the first game, the Turks seemed to want to confront Beckham on the issue of his masculinity – presumably as his hair was now in its Alice band/Flexicomb phase.

The younger Beckham may have been riled by this provocation, the older, mature captain Becks just became more determined. England deservedly got their draw, and were through to Euro 2004 in Portugal.

David Beckham's reputation was reaching a

THE BECKS A MAN CAN GET

new peak. Becks had sailed through the latest challenges in his career. However, the challenge of having his family settled in a foreign country was another matter. First of all there was Brooklyn, now settled in a top private school near the family house in Hertfordshire – it meant tearing him away from that. More significantly, perhaps, were Posh's own work commitments – and the fact she was spending more time in New York with Damon Dash, finishing her album.

Then the rumours began that Posh did not like the Spanish capital – Milan, Italy's fashion capital, had always been her first choice. She preferred to stay in England. In the first 80 days of his time at Real Madrid, she had spent only 30 or so days with Becks in Spain. Becks, it seems, was now travelling even greater distances to spend time with his family. In fact, he was also spending quite a lot of time in Madrid, left to his own devices.

Not surprisingly the popular English press was not slow to pick up on this, and in describing a "marriage crisis" between Posh and Becks. Stories of discord in the Beckham marriage continued to appear towards the end of 2003, to the point where the couple were forced to release a statement rubbishing the claims. Then in December came the

THE BECKS A MAN CAN GET

news that David had ended his association with his sporting Management Company SFX, and his agent of many years standing, Tony Stephens. Instead Becks was joining Posh at Simon Fuller's company 19. This seemed to come out of the blue.

As 2003 became 2004 there were the rumours of Becks leaving Real Madrid and returning to England. This seemed far-fetched, except that, of course, Posh did not want to move to Spain.

As it happened, Real Madrid's season was beginning to look less than glorious, when in March their chance of a Spanish Treble were dashed by losing the Spanish Cup final to Real Zaragoza, 3–2. Becks scored Madrid's opener, from a free kick, and hit the post with another, but now with the side pursuing an even more attack-minded formation Becks was now forced to assume a more defensive, holding position in midfield. This setback was followed by calamity when Real were sensationally dumped from the Champions League by Monaco in the quarter finals. Becks actually missed the crucial second leg, which Real lost 3–1, due to suspension.

By that time Posh and Becks were confronted by an even bigger bombshell than that. On April 4 2004, the *News Of the World* printed the "revelations" that gripped the country for weeks –

THE BECKS A MAN CAN GET

the Rebecca Loos story, which probably turned Victoria Beckham's life into a kind of living hell.

And as for Becks? With his PR team he has devised a strategy of smiles and silence and seems to be winning. Once more he is facing down the opposition.

In the days after the Loos kiss-and-tell story broke a PR expert wrote: "New hair styles all round, especially for David, will be fundamental to driving the sort of pictures the PR strategy will require to reassure global markets of the couple's continuing media currency." Sure enough a couple of weeks later as Posh and Becks arrive for a big birthday party for their management company 19, Becks has a new haircut – a skinhead cut very similar to his first major hairstyle change that followed his first major bust-up with Alex Ferguson in 2000.

And a few days later it is revealed that Gillette have signed Becks to endorse their range of shaving gear for a reported figure that dwarves all of his other sponsorship deals: £40 million. Maybe the Loos business has actually helped to improve his macho image. Can Becks do no wrong?

Then, there are other matters to deal with, like his football. The stakes remain huge, both with Real Madrid trying to rescue their season by

THE BECKS A MAN CAN GET

winning La Liga, and with England at Euro 2004 – perhaps the country's best chance of winning a trophy since 1966. This is Becks' opportunity to drive England to glory, and he knows it.

In short, he is still a footballer, and it is his well-paid job and wonderful good fortune to be able to go back to what he really does best: strike a football with that glorious right foot. Because it is the football which is still the most crucial part of his fame. It is the part where, time and again he has shown his brilliance, his ability to rise to the big occasion.

But as, with all sportsmen, the sword of Damocles hangs over him. Injury could end his career tomorrow. And if he were to somehow fail out on the pitch the public's appetite for him could dramatically change – as Becks knows full well.

Now 29-years-old, Becks is probably at the peak of his powers as a player. But after Euro 2004 what happens then? Does he stay at Real Madrid or does he return home to play in England with Chelsea? How long can he remain a world class player and England captain?

And in a few years time when it is all over.... what then?

BIOGRAPHIES

OTHER BOOKS IN THE SERIES

Also available in the series:

OTHER BOOKS IN THE SERIES

JENNIFER ANISTON

She's been a Friend to countless millions worldwide, and overcame numerous hurdles to rise to the very top of her field. From a shy girl with a dream of being a famous actress, through being reduced to painting scenery for high school plays, appearing in a series of flop TV shows and one rather bad movie, Jennifer Aniston has persevered, finally finding success at the very top of the TV tree.

Bringing the same determination that got her a part on the world's best-loved TV series to her attempts at a film career, she's also worked her way from rom-com cutie up to serious, respected actress and box office draw, intelligently combining indie, cult and comedy movies into a blossoming career which looks set to shoot her to the heights of Hollywood's A-list. She's also found love with one of the world's most desirable men. Is Jennifer Aniston the ultimate Hollywood Renaissance woman? It would seem she's got more than a shot at such a title, as indeed, she seems to have it all, even if things weren't always that way. Learn all about Aniston's rise to fame in this compelling biography.

OTHER BOOKS IN THE SERIES

GEORGE CLOONEY

The tale of George Clooney's astonishing career is an epic every bit as riveting as one of his blockbuster movies. It's a story of tenacity and determination, of fame and infamy, a story of succeeding on your own terms regardless of the risks. It's also a story of emergency rooms, batsuits, tidal waves and killer tomatoes, but let's not get ahead of ourselves.

Born into a family that, by Sixties' Kentucky standards, was dripping with show business glamour, George grew up seeing the hard work and heartache that accompanied a life in the media spotlight.

By the time stardom came knocking for George Clooney, it found a level-headed and mature actor ready and willing to embrace the limelight, while still indulging a lifelong love of partying and practical jokes. A staunchly loyal friend and son, a bachelor with a taste for the high life, a vocal activist for the things he believes and a born and bred gentleman; through failed sitcoms and blockbuster disasters, through artistic credibility and box office success, George Clooney has remained all of these things...and much, much more. Prepare to meet Hollywood's most fascinating megastar in this riveting biography.

OTHER BOOKS IN THE SERIES

BILLY CONNOLLY

In a 2003 London Comedy Poll to find Britain's favourite comedian, Billy Connolly came out on top. It's more than just Billy Connolly's all-round comic genius that puts him head and shoulders above the rest. Connolly has also proved himself to be an accomplished actor with dozens of small and big screen roles to his name. In 2003, he could be seen in *The Last Samurai* with Tom Cruise.

Connolly has also cut the mustard in the USA, 'breaking' that market in a way that chart-topping pop groups since The Beatles and the Stones have invariably failed to do, let alone mere stand-up comedians. Of course, like The Beatles and the Stones, Billy Connolly has been to the top of the pop charts too with D.I.V.O.R.C.E. in 1975.

On the way he's experienced heartache of his own with a difficult childhood and a divorce of his own, found the time and energy to bring up five children, been hounded by the press on more than one occasion, and faced up to some considerable inner demons. But Billy Connolly is a survivor. Now in his 60s, he's been in show business for all of 40 years, and 2004 finds him still touring. This exciting biography tells the story an extraordinary entertainer.

OTHER BOOKS IN THE SERIES

ROBERT DE NIRO

Robert De Niro is cinema's greatest chameleon. Snarling one minute, smirking the next, he's straddled Hollywood for a quarter of a century, making his name as a serious character actor, in roles ranging from psychotic taxi drivers to hardened mobsters. The scowls and pent-up violence may have won De Niro early acclaim but, ingeniously, he's now playing them for laughs, poking fun at the tough guy image he so carefully cultivated. Ever the perfectionist, De Niro holds nothing back on screen, but in real life he is a very private man – he thinks of himself as just another guy doing a job. Some job, some guy. There's more to the man than just movies. De Niro helped New York pick itself up after the September 11 terrorist attacks on the Twin Towers by launching the TriBeCa Film Festival and inviting everyone downtown. He runs several top-class restaurants and has dated some of the most beautiful women in the world, least of all supermodel Naomi Campbell. Now in his 60s, showered with awards and a living legend, De Niro's still got his foot on the pedal. There are six, yes six, films coming your way in 2004. In this latest biography, you'll discover all about his latest roles and the life of this extraordinary man.

OTHER BOOKS IN THE SERIES

MICHAEL DOUGLAS

Douglas may have been a shaggy-haired member of a hippy commune in the Sixties but just like all the best laidback, free-loving beatniks, he's gone on to blaze a formidable career, in both acting and producing.

In a career that has spanned nearly 40 years so far, Douglas has produced a multitude of hit movies including the classic *One Flew Over The Cuckoo's Nest* and *The China Syndrome* through to box office smashes such as *Starman* and *Face/Off*.

His acting career has been equally successful – from *Romancing The Stone* to *Wall Street* to *Fatal Attraction*, Douglas's roles have shown that he isn't afraid of putting himself on the line when up there on the big screen.

His relationship with his father; his stay in a top clinic to combat his drinking problem; the breakdown of his first marriage; and his publicised clash with the British media have all compounded to create the image of a man who's transformed himself from being the son of Hollywood legend Kirk Douglas, into Kirk Douglas being the dad of Hollywood legend, Michael Douglas.

OTHER BOOKS IN THE SERIES

HUGH GRANT

He's the Oxford fellow who stumbled into acting, the middle-class son of a carpet salesman who became famous for bumbling around stately homes and posh weddings. The megastar actor who claims he doesn't like acting, but has appeared in over 40 movies and TV shows.

On screen he's romanced a glittering array of Hollywood's hottest actresses, and tackled medical conspiracies and the mafia. Off screen he's hogged the headlines with his high profile girlfriend as well as finding lifelong notoriety after a little Divine intervention in Los Angeles.

Hugh Grant is Britain's biggest movie star, an actor whose talent for comedy has often been misjudged by those who assume he simply plays himself.

From bit parts in Nottingham theatre, through comedy revues at the Edinburgh Fringe, and on to the top of the box office charts, Hugh has remained constant – charming, witty and ever so slightly sarcastic, obsessed with perfection and performance while winking to his audience as if to say: "This is all awfully silly, isn't it?" Don't miss this riveting biography.

OTHER BOOKS IN THE SERIES

NICOLE KIDMAN

On 23 March 2003 Nicole Kidman won the Oscar for Best Actress for her role as Virginia Woolf in *The Hours.* That was the night that marked Nicole Kidman's acceptance into the upper echelons of Hollywood royalty. She had certainly come a long way from the 'girlfriend' roles she played when she first arrived in Hollywood – in films such as *Billy Bathgate* and *Batman Forever* – although even then she managed to inject her 'pretty girl' roles with an edge that made her acting stand out. And she was never merely content to be Mrs Cruise, movie star's wife. Although she stood dutifully behind her then husband in 1993 when he was given his star on the Hollywood Walk of Fame, Nicole got a star of her own 10 years later, in 2003.

Not only does Nicole Kidman have stunning good looks and great pulling power at the box office, she also has artistic credibility. But Nicole has earned the respect of her colleagues, working hard and turning in moving performances from a very early age. Although she dropped out of school at 16, no one doubts the intelligence and passion that are behind the fiery redhead's acting career, which includes television and stage work, as well as films. Find out how Kidman became one of Hollywood's most respected actresses in this compelling biography.

OTHER BOOKS IN THE SERIES

MICHAEL JACKSON

Friday 29 August 1958 was not a special day in Gary, Indiana, and indeed Gary, was far from being a special place. But it was on this day and in this location that the world's greatest entertainer was to be born, Michael Joseph Jackson.

The impact that this boy was destined to have on the world of entertainment could never have been estimated. Here we celebrate Michael Jackson's extraordinary talents, and plot the defining events over his 40-year career. This biography explores the man behind the myth, and gives an understanding of what drives this special entertainer.

In 1993, there was an event that was to rock Jackson's world. His friendship with a 12-year-old boy and the subsequent allegations resulted in a lawsuit, a fall in record sales and a long road to recovery. Two marriages, three children and 10 years later there is a feeling of déjà vu as Jackson again deals with more controversy. Without doubt, 2004 proves to be the most important year in the singer's life. Whatever that future holds for Jackson, his past is secured, there has never been and there will never again be anything quite like Michael Jackson.

OTHER BOOKS IN THE SERIES

JENNIFER LOPEZ

There was no suggestion that the Jennifer Lopez of the early Nineties would become the accomplished actress, singer and icon that she is today. Back then she was a dancer on the popular comedy show *In Living Color* – one of the Fly Girls, the accompaniment, not the main event. In the early days she truly was Jenny from the block; the Bronx native of Puerto Rican descent – another hopeful from the east coast pursuing her dreams in the west.

Today, with two marriages under her belt, three multi-platinum selling albums behind her and an Oscar-winning hunk as one of her ex-boyfriends, she is one of the most talked about celebrities of the day. Jennifer Lopez is one of the most celebrated Hispanic actresses of all time.

Her beauty, body and famous behind, are lusted after by men and envied by women throughout the world. She has proven that she can sing, dance and act. Yet her critics dismiss her as a diva without talent. And the criticisms are not just about her work, some of them are personal. But what is the reality? Who is Jennifer Lopez, where did she come from and how did get to where she is now? This biography aims to separate fact from fiction to reveal the real Jennifer Lopez.

OTHER BOOKS IN THE SERIES

MADONNA

Everyone thought they had Madonna figured out in early 2003. The former Material Girl had become Maternal Girl, giving up on causing controversy to look after her two children and set up home in England with husband Guy Ritchie. The former wild child had settled down and become respectable. The new Madonna would not do anything to shock the establishment anymore, she'd never do something like snogging both Britney Spears and Christina Aguilera at the MTV Video Music Awards... or would she?

Of course she would. Madonna has been constantly reinventing herself since she was a child, and her ability to shock even those who think they know better is both a tribute to her business skills and the reason behind her staying power. Only Madonna could create gossip with two of the current crop of pop princesses in August and then launch a children's book in September. In fact, only Madonna would even try.

In her 20-year career she has not just been a successful pop singer, she is also a movie star, a business woman, a stage actress, an author and a mother. Find out all about this extraordinary modern-day icon in this new compelling biography.

OTHER BOOKS IN THE SERIES

BRAD PITT

From the launch pad that was his scene stealing turn in *Thelma And Louise* as the sexual-enlightening bad boy. To his character-driven performances in dramas such as *Legends of the Fall* through to his Oscar-nominated work in *Twelve Monkeys* and the dark and razor-edged Tyler Durden in *Fight Club*, Pitt has never rested on his laurels. Or his good looks.

And the fact that his love life has garnered headlines all over the world hasn't hindered Brad Pitt's profile away from the screen either – linked by the press to many women, his relationships with the likes of Juliette Lewis and Gwyneth Paltrow. Then of course, in 2000, we had the Hollywood fairytale ending when he tied the silk knot with Jennifer Aniston.

Pitt's impressive track record as a superstar, sex symbol *and* credible actor looks set to continue as he has three films lined up for release over the next year – as Achilles in the Wolfgang Peterson-helmed Troy; Rusty Ryan in the sequel *Ocean's Twelve* and the titular Mr Smith in the thriller *Mr & Mrs Smith* alongside Angelina Jolie. Pitt's ever-growing success shows no signs of abating. Discover all about Pitt's meteoric rise from rags to riches in this riveting biography.

OTHER BOOKS IN THE SERIES

SHANE RICHIE

Few would begrudge the current success of 40-year-old Shane Richie. To get where he is today, Shane has had a rather bumpy roller coaster ride that has seen the hard working son of poor Irish immigrants endure more than his fair share of highs and lows – financially, professionally and personally.

In the space of four decades he has amused audiences at school plays, realised his childhood dream of becoming a Pontins holiday camp entertainer, experienced homelessness, beat his battle with drink, became a million-aire then lost the lot. He's worked hard and played hard.

When the producers of *EastEnders* auditioned Shane for a role in the top TV soap, they decided not to give him the part, but to create a new character especially for him. That character was Alfie Moon, manager of the Queen Vic pub, and very quickly Shane's TV alter ego has become one of the most popular soap characters in Britain. This biography is the story of a boy who had big dreams and never gave up on turning those dreams into reality.

OTHER BOOKS IN THE SERIES

JONNY WILKINSON

"There's 35 seconds to go, this is the one. It's coming back for Jonny Wilkinson. He drops for World Cup glory. It's over! He's done it! Jonny Wilkinson is England's Hero yet again..."

That memorable winning drop kick united the nation, and lead to the start of unprecedented victory celebrations throughout the land. In the split seconds it took for the ball to leave his boot and slip through the posts, Wilkinson's life was to change forever. It wasn't until three days later, when the squad flew back to Heathrow and were met with a rapturous reception, that the enormity of their win, began to sink in.

Like most overnight success stories, Wilkinson's journey has been a long and dedicated one. He spent 16 years 'in rehearsal' before achieving his finest performance, in front of a global audience of 22 million, on that rainy evening in Telstra Stadium, Sydney.

But how did this modest self-effacing 24-year-old become England's new number one son? This biography follows Jonny's journey to international stardom. Find out how he caught the rugby bug, what and who his earliest influences were and what the future holds for our latest English sporting hero.

OTHER BOOKS IN THE SERIES

ROBBIE WILLIAMS

Professionally, things can't get much better for Robbie Williams. In 2002 he signed the largest record deal in UK history when he re-signed with EMI. The following year he performed to over 1.5 million fans on his European tour, breaking all attendance records at Knebworth with three consecutive sell-out gigs.

Since going solo Robbie Williams has achieved five number one hit singles, five number one hit albums; 10 Brits and three Ivor Novello awards. When he left the highly successful boy band Take That in 1995 his future seemed far from rosy. He got off to a shaky start. His nemesis, Gary Barlow, had already recorded two number one singles and the press had virtually written Williams off. But then in December 1997, he released his Christmas single, *Angels.*

Angels re-launched his career – it remained in the Top 10 for 11 weeks. Since then Robbie has gone from strength to strength, both as a singer and a natural showman. His live videos are a testament to his performing talent and his promotional videos are works of art.

This biography tells of Williams' journey to the top – stopping off on the way to take a look at his songs, his videos, his shows, his relationships, his rows, his record deals and his demons.